OCT **1 9** 2004

Machers and Rockers

BY RICH COHEN

Tough Jews

The Avengers

Lake Effect

Machers *and* Rockers

Machers and Rockers

Chess Records and the Business of Rock & Roll

Rich Cohen

Atlas Books

W. W. Norton & Company
New York • London

For information about permission to reproduce selections from this book,
write to Permissions, W. W. Norton & Company, Inc.
500 Fifth Avenue, New York, NY 10110

Manufacturing by The Courier Companies, Inc.
Book design by Chris Welch
Production manager: Amanda Morrison

Library of Congress Cataloging-in-Publication Data

Cohen, Rich.
Machers and rockers : Chess Records and the business of rock & roll / Rich
Cohen.—1st ed.
p. cm.—(Enterprise)
"Atlas Books."
Includes bibliographical references (p.   ) and index.
ISBN 0-393-05280-X (hardcover)
1. Chess, Leonard, 1917– 2. Chess, Phil, 1921– 3. Sound recording execu-
tives and producers—Illinois—Chicago—Biography. 4. Chess Records (Firm)
I. Title. II. Enterprise (New York, N.Y.)
ML405.C63 2004
781.66'0973—dc22
2004011792

W. W. Norton & Company, Inc., 500 Fifth Avenue, New York, N.Y. 10110
www.wwnorton.com

W. W. Norton & Company Ltd.
Castle House, 75/76 Wells Street, London W1T 3QT

1 2 3 4 5 6 7 8 9 0

To my brother Steven Michael Cohen,
for giving me his record collection,
and the good room

Contents

Machers and Rockers

1

Today You Are a Man, Go Get Me a Drink

Marshall Chess was laughing it up. It was supposed to be a holy affair, the day when thirteen-year-old Marshall reads from the Torah and becomes a man (he had been dreading the day since fifth grade), but the view from the bima was lunacy—a comical clash of hairstyles and fashions, bouffants and Afros, fedoras and porkpie hats. Up front were aunts and uncles, friends and hangers-on from the community of Jews that once filled the low-slung houses around Maxwell Street, on the West Side of Chicago, an open-air market of pushcarts and fruit stands, muggy-faced women in pirate-sized rings and furs, each sentence closed with the word *bee-you-tee-full*. The men wore dark hats and itchy suits, the wind still sharp in these first weeks of April, 1955. Polish immigrants with memories of pogroms, schnorrers whose slumped shoulders whisper, *Don't mind me, I'm not even here*. They had come to pay homage to Leonard Chess, the father of the bar mitzvah boy and the great star of the old block, a gruff, ambitious man who spoke in the unapologetic way of the slum. *Where the fuck is this fucking rabbi? Get this cocksucker in here and let's do this fucking thing.*

A decade before, Leonard had been working behind the counter of a South Side liquor store. Each night, black dandies came in from the factories and slaughter yards, bought a bottle of Ripple or Old Crow, which they drank in back, laughing and goofing. Now and then, someone came in with a guitar or harmonica and pounded through one of the old songs from the South, maybe a fast, dirty version of "Big Legged Woman":

> *You got a big legged woman, boys, pin her to your side*
> *She holds up her thumb, you bound to let her ride*

Leonard developed a taste for this music, but mostly he had a head for business, what the front-row Jews called a Yiddische kupp, a Jew's brain. In the rough rhythm, he heard the jingle of cash registers. He borrowed money from his father and—with his kid brother and lifelong business partner, Phil—opened the Macomba Lounge, at 2305 South Cottage Grove, in the center of what the locals called the Black Belt and what the newspapers called Bronzeville. The club had a jumpy house band. The best musicians in town would swing by after hours, when the other clubs had closed for the night. When record scouts began haunting the Macomba, signing and recording Leonard's acts, he figured, *What the hell,* and began recording them himself. This was the genesis of Chess Records, which, over the course of its peak years, from 1948 to 1968, became one of the great engines of American life, a creator of teen culture, a presser of race records that crossed over into the mainstream. By the mid-fifties, the company had released or distributed handfuls of hits, including "Can't Be Satisfied" by Muddy Waters, "Rocket 88" by Ike Turner, "At Last" by Etta James, "I'm a Man" by Bo Diddley, and "Maybellene" by Chuck Berry.

It can be argued that Leonard Chess, along with a handful of the musicians he signed and promoted and coddled and fucked over and enriched, invented the very idea of Rock & Roll. There was Muddy Waters, who set the basic back beat and pose: "I got a black cat bone, got the mojo too, got seven hundred dollars, gonna mess with you." Willie Dixon, who wrote many of the songs and claimed one need not suffer to write about suffering: "A man don't have to be starving to know how it feels," he said. "All he's got to do is miss two meals." Little Walter, who, with his amplified harmonica, conjured the jazzy sunglasses at night groove. And later Chuck Berry, who retooled the Blues into a racy machine that could run on the preoccupations of the white teenager: "American history and practical math, study them hard and hope to pass." It was a fast-paced sound, coming into the city on a Friday afternoon, the sound of Chess but also the sound of Chicago—"Juke," say, Muddy's jumpy guitar punctuated by the wail of Little Walter on harmonica, or else for thematic reasons call it a Jew's harp, the musician cupping it in his big hand, blasting the groove that makes you think of the city in the winter, the roads frozen, the lake just a sheet of glass.

At the time of the bar mitzvah, Chess had two hundred employ-

ees, a studio at 2120 South Michigan Avenue, and a team of
scouts scouring the country for talent. It was a golden moment.
Each year, the label released around 200 new records, with sales
in the neighborhood of three million dollars. Elvis Presley had
recently made his first national TV appearance (the Dorsey
Brothers' "Stage Show"), bringing the sound created at Chess to
the millions, setting a fire that would burn through the century.
But mostly it was a business, like garments or diamonds, only
songs—*who knew you could strike it rich with a few schvartzas
and a reel-to-reel?* And good enough to take Leonard out of the
slums, up the lake to the suburbs, to Glencoe, an old money
town that, until a few years before, had been largely closed to
Jews. Leonard was Jackie Robinson, opening the North Shore to
the Hebrews—who can think of a more exotic first soldier on
the beach? He smoked, shouted, talked with his hands, joked,
laughed. He drove a Cadillac. He built a barbecue pit where he
cooked steaks for Muddy Waters and Chuck Berry. He was a
harbinger, the first of a legion of white men who would cross the
racial divide in search of riches, adventure, authenticity.

In the middle of the schul were the sort of guests that tempt
a cheapie like Leonard to write off the whole affair as a business
expense. Producers, engineers, DJs, most on the take, pressers
and promoters, but also competitors, independent record men
who, along with Leonard and Phil Chess, made up that first generation of Rock & Roll executives. These men, some at the bar
mitzvah, some not, were mostly Jews, men who, a generation
before, might have run with gangsters, who, a generation later,
might have worked on Wall Street—Harvey Weinstein types who

grew up in homes where Yiddish was the first language:

Sid Nathan—the cigar-smoking cannonball who founded King Records in Cincinatti. Nathan signed James Brown, so whenever a black kid bought "Say It Loud, I'm Black and I'm Proud," Sidney got his cut.

Hy Weiss—the founder of Bang Records, a tough runner out of the Bronx, great to have around because he said things like *How do you celebrate a hit? You go to the bank, schmuck.*

Ahmet Ertegun and Jerry Wexler—the Turk and the Jew, who built the only independent label that outclassed Chess: Atlantic— Ray Charles, Aretha Franklin, Joe Turner, Bobby Darin. To the men in the room, Ertegun and Wexler were the original record men, and about the biggest compliment you could give a guy was to call him a record man, to say he had an ear, was one of that fraternity who could spot a hit. In a sour mood, a competitor might say, *Yeah, Ahmet's got a great ear—it just happens to be attached to Jerry's head.*

In the sixties, Wexler went all out, turned up at conventions in wide lapels, madras shirts, sandals. But back then he was still clean-cut, the suit in a room of jazzed-up junkies. His stories were legend: catching a ferry from New Orleans to Algiers, a get-beat-up-and-mugged sort of place. The white cabby stopping at the edge of a field, pointing to distant lights, saying, "I ain't going to that nigger town." Wexler proceeding on foot, symbolic of the journey made by all true record men. Reaching a shack, music blasting. Someone shouting *Cop!* when he walked in. Losing himself in the strange piano of Professor Longhair, who ran his fingers all over the keys.

"You won't believe this," Wexler told the musician. "But I want to record you."

"You won't believe *this*," said Professor Longhair. "But I just signed with Mercury."

To Wexler, Leonard Chess was a provincial, a vulgar operator, but he had an ear. He was a record man. "Some view [the brothers] as crass," Wexler wrote in his autobiography, *Rhythm & the Blues: A Life in American Music*. "Some are put off by their Yiddish-inflected speech and sell-sell-sell sensibility. Personally, I love them. They're not polished producers, but they put out blistering sides. Their roster is spectacular, the finest blues repository in history."

Near the back of the schul was the next generation, the sons and grandsons of the slump-shouldered Jews up front. Doctors, lawyers, professionals who prompt a memory of the old joke about the yenta running down the beach, shouting, "Help, my son the doctor is drowning." In them you could already see the end of the story, the passing away of the old life, the deli culture our fathers exchanged for houses in suburbia, each lost in its green carpet of lawn. Basketball in the driveway, Hebrew school twice a week, the city just a storm on the horizon. They were better looking than their parents, bigger and stronger and better fed, like genetically engineered tomatoes, but not half as tasty. They spoke with the nasal whine of the Midwest, and, unlike the first generation, did not have to try to disappear; they were already gone, vanished into brown suits and gray houses, fading away and over the wall, no struggle, no adventure, no stories, even the trip to the schul experienced as a reckless jaunt into dangerous territory. To such young men, Leonard stood out as a pirate: rather than steer clear of the ghetto, this bastard actually worked there, on the South Side, with the wildest elements of the city.

But in the last row, that's where the real action was—the engine that set the whole thing running. Singers and songwriters and harp players and guitarists and bass players and drummers—black dudes set like a thumping bass line at the bottom of the song, *boom, boom, boom,* electric suits and parrot-colored neckties and two-tone loafers, a splash of color in a monochrome world. That's what got Marshall laughing—all these old Jews backed by a privet hedge of Afros and conked hair—each time one of these guys leans back, he leaves a stain on the chair—yarmulkes on top, like the cherry on the ice cream sundae. Looking across the sanctuary, Marshall can track his father's entire journey: from the Jews of his youth to the sharpies of the business world to the black artists that made it all possible. Muddy Waters and Jimmy Rogers and Otis Spann. These men worked with Leonard but came for Marshall, little Marshall the mascot. He would sit on a stool in the studio, absorbing the music and language and style as these men laid down the tracks that would define an era.

What Marshall remembers most is the smell. "Guys sweatin' and playin' in the summer. Muddy in one of those sleeveless T-shirts, the funk." Marshall speaks of his first meeting with Muddy the way a Brazilian might speak of a childhood encounter with Pelé. Marshall was eight, playing in the yard, when a black Cadillac glided to the curb. The door swung open, the hinges creaked, and out stepped this huge man, grinning like crazy, hair teased into a three-inch pompadour, buckskin shoes with fur tongues. He grabbed Marshall's arm and said, "You must be little Chess!" After that, Marshall called Muddy grandfather. Muddy's wife often sent Marshall fried chicken in foil. When Marshall was trying to woo a girl, Muddy helped by writing a poem, which Marshall passed on to the girl. It was quite dirty. When Marshall was in high school, Chess guitarist Buddy Guy fixed him a mojo, a pink bag wound with bristly horsehair, which Marshall wore on his lapel—a voodoo trick that, as Buddy put it, "Would get those girls clinging all over your action."

It was in honor of these men that Marshall picked his bar mitzvah suit—a getup stitched by Max the Tailor, the Jew who did work for all the dandies in the Black Belt. Green gabardine, no-fly pants, broad collar inset with wire so you could roll it under like a spit curl. Sharp. Marshall would spend his life around these men and so had a kind of ease in black America that, for a white American, is entirely unusual. A few years later, during a break from college, Marshall went on the road with Bo Diddley. In South Carolina, a member of Diddley's band jumped into the crowd and white girls started to dance around him and it almost started a riot. The police moved in with clubs. One of the cops grabbed Marshall and shouted, "Nigger-loving Jew." And that pretty much nails it. *Nigger-loving Jew.* It describes every record man in the room. And the musicians were just a bunch of kike-loving niggers. And so this is the story of kikes and niggers, immigrants from Poland and Mississippi, rejects from proper society who found each other on their trip through a dark room.

The temple was Anse Motel. Most of its members had emigrated from the same town in Poland, where many of them had worked the same trade. For this reason, it was known as the "carpenters' schul." But these men had moved away from the neighborhood and came back only for special events. The streets, which had once seemed the soul of the community, were awash in new immigrants, blacks and Puerto Ricans. The Jewish presence survived only in the old temples and shops, in the ghostly Hebrew letters carved over the doors, in street names that no longer made sense: the black kids who played guitar on Maxwell, for reasons they probably did not understand, still called it Jew Street.

Marshall finished reading from the Torah, and the Ark—the home of the holy scrolls, a phone line direct to God (and you always suspect the big man has you on speaker)—was closed. The reception was a fifteen-minute drive across town—a procession of Cadillacs and Chevys snaking through gray streets to the Cotillion Room at the Morrison Hotel—beyond swank. Prayers, food, toasts, and the dance floor where a boozy uncle hands you a Tom Collins and says, *Today you are a man.* The Flamingos, a doo-wop group, one of Leonard's discoveries, is performing. Everyone crowds close to the stage, black and white, waiters with trays, chair dancers and schlomos and old Bettys—*give me a kiss, give me a kiss*—making their way through the cashmere and crinoline to Marshall, to regard him at arm's length and slip him an envelope, homage to the young prince—*Don't you know all bar mitzvah boys gauge success by the size of the take?*—a wedding scene in a mob movie, cash, coins and

Israel bonds, each decorated with a tree that will surely be planted in that desert country. But Marshall knows that his real reward will only come later, will in fact be the company itself, Chess Records, the singers and the groove, a world he will inherit.

2

Jew Street

Leonard Chess was one of those Americans whose life, the sweep of it, would have struck his ancestors as a fairy tale. He ended on the far side of the ocean, in a house a few blocks from a great inland sea, driving roads that, a generation before, had been Indian trails, his fortune made in partnership with the descendants of African slaves. He began in a world older than his great-grandfather, the shtetl-land of Eastern Europe, a town called Motel. As long as anyone could remember, the Chess family had been merchants, rag pickers, junk collectors. The family went by the name Czyz. Every few generations, when a member of the family gathered some wealth, which came and went as capriciously as wildflowers, a tavern or nightclub was opened. For this reason, the family had a sense of itself as entertainers. Leonard's father, Joseph, was short and broad, a little man who surprises you with a vicelike handshake. He worked as a peddler, traveling shtetl to shtetl, Willie Lowmanstein, out there on a shoe shine and a smile.

In the years just after the First World War, the sharpest Jews of Motel could sense a change in the weather. It was time to get out. It was a question only of destination: America or Palestine, mind or spirit, commerce or faith. Many who chose America later said Palestine was the choice of the crazies, the ideologues, the true believers. To a practical man like Joe Chess, the only direction was west. He left for Chicago in 1924, far-off city of rum-running capones, where he had an uncle. In 1928, he sent for his family.

The wife, the girls, Phil, who was five, and Leonard, twelve—old enough to have a personality, memories of life as Lezjor Czyz. He spoke Yiddish and Polish. On his left leg was a brace, the result of a childhood illness. It gave him a herky-jerky, here-comes-the-Jew gimp quality that was not selling. (As in *these records are not selling, let's move them to the back of the store.*) The family traveled to Warsaw by train—one of those European numbers chugging around a curved track, wandering past picturesque towns full of haters, a premonition of boxcars that would later take those left behind to Treblinka and Auschwitz. The family sailed to Southampton, England, where they boarded an ocean liner to New York. Five days across, each the same nothing, the wasted background of maritime paintings, nothing until nothing ends in nothing. And then, like a miracle, the towers of Manhattan rise up from the sea like magic rocks, towers and spires, the streets filled with men oblivious to your struggle, especially if you are a small boy who, until ten days before, had seen nothing and now had seen everything. On Ellis Island, the family was swept along with thousands of immigrants, accents and smells mingling in the brick halls. When Celia Chess saw people wait-ing in lines to be examined by doctors, she panicked. *Lezjor, Lezjor, your leg, the brace, they will never let you in. Go, throw it off, get rid of it.* Leonard fell in with the crowds, unhooked the brace, let it slide to the floor, stepped out of it and walked away. He never wore it again—cast off like the stink of the Old World. This casting away of the brace is, in the story of Leonard, a liter-ary symbol—it represents the reinvention of the self, the death of Lezjor Czyz and the birth of Leonard Chess, American.

The family spent the night in New York and in the morning left for Chicago, a train trip that took them out where the real country began, beyond the mills, past the weather-beaten towns of Pennsylvania, backed by gloomy Poconos, smoky cities and one-street towns where Jews don't get killed, tremendous Ohio farms and immense grassland prairies—a trip that, in the epic of Rock & Roll, runs parallel to the trip Muddy Waters would take from the Mississippi Delta to Chicago, which, in psychic dis-tance, was just as great. Railroads changed the way towns are approached, how they make their first appearance in your life. No longer can you take a place unaware; every arrival is now on schedule and every trip in the back way, as the tracks are laid far from the main thoroughfares, and the areas around the tracks surrounded by warehouses and pawnshops and flops. The train swept along Lake Michigan, through the furnace of Gary and Hammond, over rooftops and bridges, Chicago spreading out like a stain, smokestacks and stockyards, on and on, endless. And *whooosh!* The train dives into the tunnel that marks the final approach, lights flashing, conductor walking through the cars,

the hiss of air brakes, and just like that the family is lost in cav-
ernous Union Station on State Street. And here comes Joe Chess,
strong as a tree stump, smelling of coffee and cigarettes, laughing, *We made it, we made it,* taking each child up into his arms,
one after another, the girls, Leonard, then Phil, who had never
known the old man, having been just one year old when Joe left.
"Des es di tata," Celia Chess tells him. *Des es di tata—this is your
father.*

CHICAGO IS THE great American city. New York has a foot in
Europe, and Washington is a bureaucracy, and Boston is so over
it's over being over, but Chicago is the real product of the nation,
the big town on the plain, no reason for being other than a
chance to get rich. It's an Indian word: *Chickagou.* It means
"the place with the bad smell." And just wait until the wind
shifts and brings the stink from the yards! Dreiser, Anderson,
Sinclair—it's where a writer goes to plumb the depths of the
Republic. "City of big shoulders," wrote Carl Sandburg, "tool
maker, stacker of wheat, husky, brawling . . . a bold slugger set
vivid against the little soft cities." It burned down. It was built
again. Its hotels are palaces, its slums evil, "painted women
under gas lamps luring the farm boys." Punishing winters, smoky
rooms, people friendly because people drunk. Jazzy years of
Prohibition, each block controlled by a gang, Irish or Italian,
even Jews. Nails Morton, who joined the war against Al Capone,
was known as "the man who made the West Side safe for the
Yids." After years of battle, Nails was killed in Lincoln Park—

bucked, then kicked in the head, by a horse. Members of his gang led the horse back to the park and whacked it. Tough town. In pictures, the city is shrouded in smoke, the tall buildings breaking through, the mills on the shore, fire escapes, twilight and rain, chimneys, corner stores, steak houses, freight yards, prize fights, the dazzle of a soft horn—music from a party you are not invited to.

By the mid-1920s, the city was crawling with Jews, second only to New York. Fifty thousand arrived in the decade before 1900. It had always been an immigrant town, Greeks, Turks, Armenians, Italians, Irish, each tucked into his own neighborhood, his own Main Street and church and saloon. The Jews had been pushed two miles west of the lake, three miles south of the Loop, over to Halstead, a sprawl of desolate streets, diners, synagogues, tailors, kosher butchers, a remake of the shtetls, lower east side of Chi. Joseph Chess settled his family on South Karlov Street, a block crowded with families from Motel, three rooms in a shared house. Leonard and Phil slept on the couch.

It was a neighborhood where either you embraced what you were or you ran away from it. On one side were poor blacks, on the other Irish and Italians. Now and then, when school let out, the Jewish neighborhood was set upon by gangs of Catholic kids. If a Jew asked why he was taking a beating, a Catholic kid might say, *Because you killed our Lord.* Leonard was one of those who never ran away, and never pretended to be someone else: this stubbornness continued into his later life in music, a world filled with Jews at once proud of their position and terrified of being called out. Maybe he was not the most observant Jew, but Leonard never forgot who he was: he was Motel, he was Joe Chess, he was Maxwell Street, he was Jewtown.

Jewtown had been built up as a buffer. As Poland was a shield between Russia and Germany, Maxwell Street was a shield between the white neighborhoods and the black ghetto, which was growing by leaps and bounds, as migrants poured in from the South. Half a million from Mississippi in ten years. Driving through the West Side was a slow fade, a downshift from old white Chicago to new Jewish Chicago to all-black Chicago. For this reason, the Jews, more than anyone else, had real contact with the blacks—lived alongside them and, where the neighborhoods overlapped, lived with them—and this gave these communities a sense of familiarity, which did not always mean a sense of respect or trust. Sometimes the person you know best is the easiest to hate. To the blacks, the Jews around Maxwell were the usurers of myth. To the Jews, the blacks were schvartzas—a Yiddish word for "black," which, as I was told by my grandmother, placed Jews years ahead of the rest of America in calling African-Americans what they wanted to be called—a cared-for but patronized class of drivers, maids, gardeners, and cooks.

This proximity was to be a deciding factor in Leonard's life. On the way home from school, if he wandered a few blocks off course, he could lose himself in the Negro streets, an Araby of horse-drawn carts and cobblestone alleys, the ghostly tracks of streetcars long since taken out of service, liquor stores, pool halls, stoops crowded with men in pinstripes, hats pulled low, hiding from someone or something, the cold wind, which charges off the lake in great trumpet blasts. On Sunday mornings, Leonard would walk along Cottage Grove, drifting with the music from the church choirs, the soaring harmonies that drive away impurities and prepare the soul for heaven. On Friday nights, on these same streets, members of these same choirs were singing dirty songs in the dives, casting off what had been so carefully earned in church, but of course you have to get dirty to get clean, have to sin to be saved. In this way, Leonard, from his first years, developed a taste for black music—church music and its worldly offshoot, the Blues. Compared to songs like "Flip, Flop, Fly," the cantors in the schul were just one more shameful tagalong from the Old World. Negro music was the pure product, an overflowing of soul, a comment on the suffering of the New World, and a relief from that suffering.

Joseph Chess worked as a carpenter, and later as a junk dealer, first out of a pushcart, another one of those poor schnorrers humping around Maxwell, but later in his own store, the Wabash Junk Shop at 2971 South State Street. Can Joseph Chess, a man who left nothing but his children behind, who did no more than carry his family out of Europe, who worked small jobs and never made much money, nor was he involved in any epic battle or love affair, a man who lived so long ago that he has moved into the second rank of the dead—not only is he gone, but so is almost everyone who really knew him—be described? There are photos, of course, and they show a stocky man in a natty suit, rigid, jug-eared, big hands, sharp eyes. But for me, Joseph Chess is a stand-in for a whole generation of grandfathers that did the heavy lifting for the Jews of America, who laid down their bodies for their descendants to walk across.

For most of Leonard's childhood, Joseph was away on the truck, away in the store, doing whatever it is fathers do, working, earning, not laughing, not fooling—none of that. For such men, you hope only there was one nice week in Florida, a week when it was supposed to rain but didn't, because life is a test and a trial, and these men knew it. Sometimes, late at night, Joseph would take Leonard for a bite, the boy eating alone with his father, an all-night diner on the West Side, the elevated train rattling overhead, an adult world of truckers and conductors and postal clerks—the men who actually keep the city running, invisible in their basements and loading bays. *Listen, Leonard, if you spend a buck, make sure you get back a buck and a half.*

High School? For Leonard, not much to tell. The usual hard life of the immigrant kid: greenhorn, accent. He only learned to speak English in his teens. Such a kid does not fall into any of the familiar pop notions of high school. On *Beverly Hills 90210*, there is no dark-eyed, Yiddish-speaking character just arrived from Poland. Leonard never built a tree house, never drove a go-cart, never visited the American-built land of adolescence. He was instead looking for a way out of a trap, a way to again throw off the brace. He worked after school and before, in the dark of early morning, when the city rattles with trucks and drunks stumble home from the dives. He delivered newspapers, worked in shops, ran errands—whatever—to bring something home to his family. The ancient burden of the big brother: take responsibility, take control, contribute, lead.

School did not end so much as simply fade into a world of work, low-paying jobs, long hours. In 1940, Joseph Chess lost his partner: hit by a car and killed. Leonard joined the junk business. Phil was at college, at Bowling Green State University on a football scholarship, but, after just three semesters, dropped out and joined the business too. It was renamed Chess & Sons. In 1941, Leonard married Revetta Sloan. He moved straight from his parents' house into his married life, from one kind of authority to another. The couple rented a walk-up on Drexel Boulevard. Marshall was born in 1942. At work, Leonard would linger in front of the shop, listening to organ music—there was a Negro church across the street. After services, the congregants stood on the steps, the women so stately they sailed away like yachts. Phil called them "the hand clappers."

In 1945, Leonard took a job at a liquor store at 5060 South State Street, in the Black Belt. It's unclear just how he came to have this job, or why he decided to leave his father's business. Phil left too, drafted into the army. He would serve the last months of the Second World War in the Aleutian Islands. (Phil married just before he shipped out). It's like a frame is missing from the film: we go straight from Leonard at the junk shop to Leonard selling booze. Cut-Rate Liquors. Flickering neon, bottles in the window, red and rosé in the aisles. At twenty-seven, he already looked like the man who would become an icon in Chicago. A sparrow hawk: lean and strong, jut cheeks, dark, watchful eyes, a nose right out of geometry. (Phil looked more like one of the Belushis, classic Chicago, hat and big fleshy grin, dare in his eyes). In photos, Leonard is often seen with his artists, Muddy or Wolf, the brains behind Pa, a head shorter, balding, letting the big fellow take the foreground but lurking in a way that suggests, *Ah, so here is the man at the wheel.*

Leonard was the kind of person you might lose in a crowd, but then he opened his mouth and out came the voice—this big voice from this little body, the voice of Meyer Lansky or Vince Lombardi, a shock and a joke, the badgering, hectoring half-time voice of the football coach—*Come on, come on, lay that motherfucker down*—but the coach at Grambling State, or some other all-black powerhouse. When Leonard learned English, he learned syntax and grammar in school, but he learned the rhythm in the Negro streets near his apartment. The result was a once-in-history hybrid, a Polish Jew with the voice of the cotton fields. He spoke black vernacular, slang and codes, and so was an unintentional precursor to all those white music executives and wannabes who would later call a nice person "dope," or say what was clearly good was "bad," or embrace a trend as "fly." *Why you frontin,' G?* On studio tapes you cannot discern the voice of Leonard from that of his artists, and this would be turned to great advantage in his career: Leonard, so it seemed to many blacks, was one of the few whites who spoke to them with understanding and respect. In fact, he spoke to them in their own voice.

From his first days at Cut-Rate, customers felt at ease with Leonard, and so, rather than go away in the night, they hung around, talking and drinking, sitting in back, where the owner set up chairs and a stereoscope, a jukebox that flashed images. Leonard came to know every part of black Chicago, mothers and grandmothers buying wine for dinner, factory workers in denim jackets and boots, gangsters and corner boys—they came from the tenements on 47th and 50th and 53rd streets, webs of wooden fire escapes, where women hung laundry and men smoked until dawn. These men said things like, *If you hit it, hit it 'til you drop it, or leave it alone*, or, *If you gonna play it, play it when it's hot.*

Like Leonard, these were immigrants: Mississippi, Alabama, Louisiana, dirt farms and no-shit towns, a nation of men who reached their prime after emancipation but before civil rights, who channeled otherwise wasted energy into bar fights, feuds, music, a great tide that rolled up from the South. Leonard saw them not as artists—artists are a dime a dozen—but as something infinitely more rare and illusive: a market. A legion of transplants who felt lost in the frozen North, who wanted a taste and comfort from home and would pay for it. Anyone can spot an artist; only a genius can spot a market where others have seen only a horde.

In his retrospective at the Metropolitan Museum, Richard Avedon showed a picture of a man who had been born a slave. The picture was taken in 1963, almost twenty years *after* Leonard took his job at Cut-Rate, where he served mostly black immigrants from the slave states. This man, as Avedon portrays him, is rough and angry, unsociable, clear-eyed, ancient and folkloric, a relic from another age, genetically no different than those who came later, yet touched by the residue of a great evil. His features are distorted, as if squeezed in a vice—the vice of history. This same sort of distortion afflicted the men Leonard served on the South Side. The past is what they had come north to escape, and yet they never really could get away from anything: no matter what they did, there it was, in their music and in their language, especially when they were drinking. The liquor store and

its product were therefore as holy as a church: the curse and the
reward, the wound and the salt in the wound, the blind spot on
the way to clarity.

Leonard sold bottle after bottle yet himself never took a drink,
and herein lies one of the great contrasts between the music executive and his artists. As a rule, most of that first generation of
Jewish record men did not drink, or drug, or do many of the really
interesting things that were a big part of the lives of their artists.
It was the sort of abstinence that fuels suspicion: *Come on,
Leonard, why won't you drink with us?* It played into one of the
classic Jewish stereotypes, unfair and bullshit, but kind of true:
that Jews don't drink. In the twenties and thirties world of the
New York gangs, for example, Jewish thugs were known as those
who stayed sober. In a police report, a cop once described Mendy
Weiss as "a hoodlum of the gargantuan type, acts with tremendous violence, smokes huge cigars, and never takes a drink."
Maybe it was old shtetl knowledge: in a hostile world, a Jew must
hang on to whatever mental edge he can muster. (In the next
generation, this would change, with Jewish executives getting
and staying as fucked-up as their most wasted artists. It was
Herzl's dream of Zionism, which, he said, would be a success
only when "Jewish police are chasing Jewish criminals.")

Leonard would learn to use sobriety to his advantage, an ace
to play against anyone with a weakness for liquor. When a contract came up for renewal, he might call an artist on the phone,
offer favorable terms, then say, "Just come on over and let's sign
this thing." He would make sure his office was well stocked with
top-drawer scotch and vodka, set out an ice bucket and tum-

blers, then duck out. When the artist turned up, Leonard's secretary, as instructed, would say, *Mr. Chess had to run out for a minute. He said to wait in his office.* As the artist steps through the door, the secretary says, *Help yourself to a drink.* An hour later, Leonard calls in and asks his secretary, *Is he drunk?* If yes, Leonard races back, apologizes, says, *We're so excited about this deal. Let's drink to it.* He fills two tumblers, raises his glass, watches the artist throw his back. Leonard then shakes his head and says, *Now, you see, well, unfortunately, ahem, and you know, I have been in with the bankers all day over this, knocking my fucking brains out, but we just can't come up with that kind of scratch— but how do you feel about white walls? I can really sweeten this deal with a boss set of tires.*

THE FIRST RESIDENT of Chicago was black, Jean Baptiste Point du Sable, a trader and trapper from Santo Domingo. In 1779, he built a log cabin where the north branch meets the south branch of the Chicago River. Fort Dearborn was built less than a mile away, where Michigan Avenue today crosses the river. The city was born as a trading post but soon grew into a commercial center, a boom so explosive you can imagine it in time-lapse photos: skunk weed giving way to a fort surrounded by tepees, giving way to trapper cabins, giving way to farmhouses, giving way to brick streets, giving way to gaslight, giving way to a modern city of steam engines and tall buildings and political campaigns and sports teams. In the Midwest, history is collapsed into a kind of concentrate.

At the end of the nineteenth century, the city reached a critical mass, took on a life of its own, began to create movements and schools, painters and writers, most of whom wrote or painted about life in the city, began to suck and seduce all the talent from the surrounding countryside—became, in other words, a kind of black hole, so dense not even light could escape. There had always been a black community in the city. In its earliest years, Chicago had been a haven for free blacks looking for a new start. It was also haunted by runaway slaves who had slipped the bonds and made their way north along the underground railroad. Fugitives might spend weeks or months hiding in the black district then forming on the South Side, an area of wide avenues and wooden houses. Runaways sang in the taverns, so that the music of the Negro South, by the great luck of geography, could even then be heard in the streets.

The first boom in black population came with the outbreak of World War I. The factories and shops were swamped with orders at the moment the immigrants stopped coming from overseas—no more masses from Scandinavia, Germany, Ireland. The tremendous need for unskilled labor drove up salaries and began to pull black workers from the South. In 1800, there were 232 blacks in Chicago. In 1900, there were thirty thousand. By Armistice Day, there were three hundred thousand. Black immigration tapered off during the Depression as jobs disappeared, but exploded with the outbreak of World War II. In 1950, there were half a million blacks in the city. Between 1940 and 1950, Mississippi lost 25 percent of its black population. Everyone was packing up and leaving, taking along musical traditions that had been handed down for generations, long before records and radio, with every kid learning to play in the style of some forgotten slave—traditions that would turn up, as if out of nowhere, on records cut on the South Side. To these blacks, poor farmers who grew up in the floodplain of the Mississippi, Chicago was the end of the ferry run, the top of the river, the last name on the big board in the Memphis train station. It suggested a longing captured in Robert Johnson's "Sweet Home Chicago," in Jimmy Rogers's "Chicago Bound," in Arthur "Big Boy" Crudup's "Chicago Blues." According to legend, Little Walter walked to the city from St. Louis. When he arrived, said Johnny Shines, "His feet were swolled up like two loaves of bread."

So why Chicago? Well, there were jobs, delivery jobs and factory jobs and warehouse jobs that paid a decent wage. In 1940, a black worker in Mississippi took home around four hundred thirty-nine dollars a year. In Chicago, the same worker could make over two grand. There was cultural pull. Chicago was the home of the *Chicago Defender,* the oldest and most influential black newspaper in the country, a muckraking broadsheet sold across the South. It made the city seem a place of sophistication and freedom. And there was the Sears catalogue, return address Chicago, a tome offering the wonders and the delicacies of the world (dresses, cosmetics, farm equipment) ordered layaway from that far-off Baghdad. The Sears catalogue is where Muddy Waters bought his first guitar.

But mostly it was the railroad, the Illinois Central, with spurs across the South leading to Chicago. In off hours, these were just iron tracks curving through a back lot or field, grass growing between the ties, something to follow into town, but once or twice a day they rattled like the pier landings of Mark Twain, the train blasting through the flats or the bayou or the pine, the engine sending up smoke, the carriages rocking, faces in the windows. For a moment, the countryside was remade as a strange vision, the train vanishing with a cry around a bend. There was the Creole, which traveled to Chicago from New Orleans via Jackson, Mississippi; there was the Lousiane, which traveled to Chicago from Greenville, Mississippi; there was the Southern Express, which traveled to Chicago from Birmingham, Alabama. To blacks in the South the train stood for freedom. It floats through dozens of tunes, appearing in old folk Blues and in city Blues and later in Rock & Roll songs written by jet-age superstars who cannot possibly understand its significance, who include it as a nod, or a tick, or a stab at authenticity—a symbol unmoored from what it is supposed to symbolize.

Sonny Boy Williamson, in "Bring It on Home": "I done bought my ticket and got my load, conductor holler 'All aboard,' take my seat way in back, and watch this train move down the track." Roy Acuff, in "Wabash Cannonball": "Listen to the rumble, the rattle and the roll, she glides along the fast plains, by the hills and by the shore." The Pixies, decades later, in "Here Comes Your Man": "Outside there's a boxcar waiting, outside the family stew, out by the fire breathing, outside we wait 'til face turns blue."

But it's more than the lyrics: it's the sound of the songs, which somehow capture the rhythm of the railroad, the clackety-clack you plug into the moment before you fall asleep on the train, sleeping deeply and waking to find yourself in a new country, the farms and fields far behind, the streets dotted with the kind of shabby liquor stores and check-cashing joints that mark the approach to cities. It's a sound and a mood that gets into these songs and stays there the way, even after a trip, the smell of the airplane stays in your clothes.

Mostly it's the idea of the railroad as the modern world, a light-filled carriage cutting through inky fields. It has turned up in our art from the beginning, the terrible power and inevitability of progress: it's the train that mangled poor Anna Karenina and that carried away the true love of Robert Johnson. In "New York City Serenade," Bruce Springsteen wrote: "She won't take the train, she's afraid them tracks are gonna slow her down." The strangeness of the trip is captured at the Art Institute in Chicago: on the first floor is a Monet painting that shows a luxury train waiting at a platform, surrounded by crowds, a scene softened by the clouds of steam that settle at the beginning of all quests; after wandering through God-knows-what blasted countryside, this very same train (so it seems to me) turns up in the modern wing, in a painting by the surrealist Magritte, emerging from the back of a fireplace. The world has dissolved like wet paper, fallen into a clash of meaningless images, but the train rattles on. As Henry David Thoreau wrote in his notebooks: "What's the railroad to me? I never go to see where it ends. It fills a few hollows and makes banks for the swallows."

In 1945, a man boarding the Creole in New Orleans at 8:30 a.m. would reach Chicago at 8:30 the following morning—a 24-hour run up the spine of America. The trip cost seventeen dollars. First sight of the city was always the same: slums, bungalows, towers, the winter sun flashing off the lake like a heliograph. "I got off that train and [Chicago] looked like the fastest place in the world," Muddy Waters said. "Cabs dropping fares, horns blowing, people walking so fast."

In *Blues People,* his angry polemic on African American Music, LeRoi Jones, now Amiri Bakara, writes of this disorientating arrival:

> To most Negroes, urban living was a completely strange idea. They had come from all over the South, from backwoods farms as sharecroppers who had never been to even moderately large cities of the South, to the fantastic metropolises of the North. It must have been almost as strange as that initial trip their ancestors made centuries before into the new world. Now the Negroes had not even the land to walk across. Everywhere was cement, buildings, the streets filled with automobiles. Whole families jammed up in tiny unbelievably dirty flats or rooming houses. But the sole idea was "to move," to split from the incredible fabric of guilt and servitude identified so graphically within the Negro consciousness of the white South.

The émigré was soon living in the slums. When the clouds rolled in, blocking the tall buildings, it could have been 1890. The picturesque decay of Steinbeck's *Cannery Row* or Naipaul's *Miguel Street.* Race relations in Chicago had always been bad. In 1919, when a black kid swam across an invisible line at the 23rd Street beach, he was set upon by a white mob and drowned,

The South Side of Chicago, April 1941, depository of the great migration, the infinite streets of the Negro slum. (© Corbis)

a murder that set off six days of rioting and left thirty-nine people dead.

Most immigrants stayed with a relative while looking for a job. In the years after the Second World War, work was plentiful and a man might find employment the day of arrival. Muddy Waters, who came from Clarksdale, Mississippi, worked in a container factory, a paper plant, and on a delivery truck. Koko Taylor, who came from Memphis, Tennessee, worked as a maid on the North Side. Jimmy Rogers, who came from Ruleville, Mississippi, worked at a chicken-processing plant, a shoe factory, and a meat-packing plant. For even successful musicians, such jobs remained a necessity. They performed in the sad now-and-then manner of wedding bands—worked in the factory or machine shop until five, dashed home, cleaned off the grime, put on fancy clothes, and headed to the clubs. These were the glory days of the South Side saloons, dozens of dance halls filling with sharpies who only wanted to party. The names of these joints read like a poem of lost Chicago: the Square Deal Club, at 230 West Division Street; the Circle Inn, at 63rd and Wentworth streets; Club Claremont, at 39th Street and Indiana Avenue; Club Georgia, at 45th and State; the Temp Tap, at 31st and Indiana Avenue; Ruby Lee's Gatewood Tavern—"the Gate"—at West Lake and North Artesian Avenue. It was all in the city at night; you just needed the nerve to take it.

In 1949, after moving from liquor store to liquor store, Leonard Chess decided to buy into the booming world of Bronzeville. With money borrowed from his father, he purchased the Congress Street Buffet, a rundown restaurant at 47th Street and South Karlov, the heart of the ghetto. Leonard and Phil rebuilt the restaurant into a nightclub, tearing out tables and countertops and classing it up, with velvet booths and a horseshoe-shaped bar, a barbecue pit, and a stage for bands. He called it the Macomba Lounge. It was so narrow, two men could not pass side by side. Yet within a few months it had grown into one of the hot spots in the city, a regular stop on the late night rounds. Leonard put together a house band that brought in the crowds as well as other musicians, who would jump on stage for a quick number. Leonard had a genuine ear for music—or at least he had an ear for what other people had an ear for. He could not necessarily spot something that was going to be big, but he could spot a new version of what had been big already. This was before the Delta Blues hit the city. Most of the clubs still featured velvet-voiced singers who danced with the microphone and enunciated, music geared to the black middle class and the white slummers who claimed to find elemental power on the wrong side of town.

The house band was led by Tommy Archia, who would blow his tenor sax like Coleman Hawkins. With a few notes, he could invoke an entire era, an era vanishing as fast as sea foam, a sophisticated just-back-from-the-war blues that could play without offense in the slickest club on the North Side. Like Hollywood movies, it was an art that had ceased to be dangerous. Archia was backed by a tight combo: word got around, and soon the Macomba was packing them in. Leonard had hit just the right chord at just the right moment. How did he do it? He was a sharp operator for one, had his finger on the pulse but never lost sight of the details. Greasing the cops, for example. Anyone can slip a fin to a crusher, but not everyone knows the exact right crusher to slip to: the cop who can see to it that the city's draconian saloon rules do not apply. The Macomba was able to stay open long after the other clubs had the chairs up on the tables. The best late-night joint in Bronzeville, Archia playing as the other joints went dark. Ella Fitzgerald, Dinah Washington, Max Roach—every hotshot swung by the Lounge.

On certain nights the club was swept up in a sort of delirium—like one of those garish old folk paintings, the bar bursting with music, the air filled with projectiles, bouncers bum-rushing heavies into the street, and everywhere the twist and shrug of arms and elbows, smiles full of teeth as Leonard goes about his serious money-making business behind the bar.

Want a drink, Leonard?

No thanks.

There was a real what-you-see-is-what-you-get naturalness to Leonard. When he was happy, he smiled. When he was sad, he frowned. If he liked someone, he said, "Him I like." If he disliked someone, he said, "Him not so much." When it came to confidential matters—how many C-notes were in the till, where the next payoff was going—Leonard and Phil spoke in code, a vocabulary of secret words that struck patrons as a kind of nonsense, but was in fact Yiddish. The use of the old language for private business goes back to the beginning of the big-money Jews and so touches on the very worst fears of Jewish conspiracy. In their great days of financial empire, the Rothschilds and the Warburgs, with brothers and cousins scattered among the banking capitals of the world, used to write communiqués in a code of Yiddish words spelled with Hebrew characters. These sentences were written, like Hebrew, right to left—a historical tidbit that echoes. You hear it in one of the greatest movies of the silent era, *Nosferatu,* the Dracula story told as a dark dream by F. W. Murnau. Dracula always struck me as a personification of the old, old anti-Semitism, a Rothschild-like count closed up in a creepy castle in Romania, a virgin-defiling, blood-sucking parasite. In the film, Nosferatu is seen writing a letter at the high desk of a number cruncher. He is hooked-nosed and pale, and laughing the cackling laughter that so taunted Hitler, but most telling is the letter itself, which is written right to left and consists of crazy Semitic-looking symbols. The Jew dominating with a gibberish of legalisms is an image that reverberates like a wah-wah pedal through the history of Rock & Roll. Talking about Morris Levy, one of the pioneering record men, Hy Weiss says, "In sit-downs, these rock musicians from England of course expected to meet this little purple-lipped Jew. Instead they found themselves across a table from this big brawler who could break them over his knee like dead wood."

According to its license, the Macomba was to close at four a.m., but if things were cooking, Leonard said, "Fuck it," or, as they say on the West Side, "Fuck that shit," pulled the shutters, closed the blinds and roared on, through the dawn, into the morning, the sun beating like a strobe across the lake. The lounge became a crossroads of drug traffic, the connection sitting at the bar like an exposed wire. Exchanges in the bathroom, in the alley, right up front, a packet of cocaine taped under a stool. After closing, Leonard and Phil would check every chair, flushing what they found. There were threats, fights, holdups. One night, a man came at Leonard with a knife. Big Gene, who worked for Leonard as a kind of bodyguard, stepped in front of the blade. It took seventy stitches to close the wound. Another night, when Leonard brought Marshall to work—he was five years old—gunfire broke out. Marshall remembers his father tossing him over the bar and lying on top of him—an incident that probably convinced Leonard there was not much future in the nightclub business.

Each morning after closing, Leonard stood in the slummy

street with a pocket full of Chivas-stained bills. The Macomba was a cash business. For protection, he wore a 44-caliber pistol outside his pants. Once in his car, he crossed the breadth of the city, heading to the havens of the South Shore, redbrick townhouses revealing their true color at first light, tenements whistling past, the blocks empty in this dead hour of delivery men and lunatics. Leonard made his deposit at the bank, then swung by the house to pick up Marshall. The day ended on the lake, father and son fishing in a little boat, the sweet cool-down after the epic night: the slosh of water, the arc of fishing lines, the reassuring stink from the factories, water so polluted the white fish were just looking for a reason to die.

Before long, a new type of patron had appeared at the Macomba: white men in dark suits who listened to bands with sharp-eyed detachment. Some carried pads and scribbled notes. Pulling Leonard aside, they would ask: "What do the people dig?" "Is Tommy Archia a good boy?" "Can you dance to it?" Leonard at first believed these men to be aficionados, experience collectors swimming ahead of the tide, but soon realized they were record men—small-time producers scouring the clubs. Leonard took an interest in these men. He served as a sort of unpaid scout, steering them to artists, watching how a record man approaches a musician, works him, then, for chump change, presses a single that can be sold in the bars, the newsstands, the drugstores.

In 1947, when Sammy Goldberg, a black scout, came after Andrew Tibbs, who now and then sang at the Macomba, Leonard had a realization: *Why recruit Andrew Tibbs so Sammy Goldberg can turn a dollar? Why not record Tibbs myself?* Leonard then made the moves that were to prove decisive: he spoke to Tibbs, convincing him, locking him into a deal, then proposed a partnership to Evelyn Aron, an acquaintance who, with her husband, Charles, owned an independent record label called Aristocrat. The Arons had the company and the experience, but Leonard had access to the talent. In other words, a great musical empire grew out of the old immigrant sensibility: *Schmucko! Why do for others what you can do for yourself? If you spend a buck, make sure you get back a buck and a half!*

WHEN LEONARD CHESS turned up on the scene, recording was still a new medium. It was a product of that late nineteenth century moment of invention that saw the mad professors hang the wallpaper of the modern world. Airplane, horseless carriage, machine gun. The first recordings were a by-product, a magnificent accident, stumbled across by Thomas Edison while looking to improve his telephone. In the coming decades, this invention was toyed with and reinvented, a great pursuit race between French and American lab rats, a history told in terms like *phonautograph, fluctuating air pressure, smoked cylinder, photoengraving, tin foil cylinder, compressed air amplifier, auxetophone, diode thermionic valve.*

In 1884, the first wire recording was made—Emile Berliner, an immigrant, reading The Lords Prayer; in 1886, Edison made the first wax recording ("Mary Had a Little Lamb"), leading the way to the modern record and all kinds of head shops with names like Hot Wax and Wax Tracks; in 1889, penny arcades in places like Coney Island began to feature coin-in-slot replay machines, early Steamboat Willie versions of the jukebox, which played speeches and sound effects; in 1902, Caruso made his first recording, a hit that proved the existence of a market; in 1903, the first twelve-inch wax record was pressed; in 1919, Paul Whiteman and his orchestra released the first million-selling record, *Japanese Sandman.* By the 1920s, the race had led to something like the modern ready-for-sale phonograph record.

Audio recording is a twin of the photograph: these inventions, taken together, were to change the way your average person processed the world. With recorded music, you could bring into your home the sound of the London Orchestra but also—and it took longer to see the value in this—the sound of cotton workers chanting in the fields. These records captured and held music that, until then, swept by as swiftly as rain, never comparable to literature if only because it could not be preserved and experienced again and again—it could only be ridden like a wave, like time itself, of which it is an expression and a metaphor. In fact, by capturing the human voice and the sound of strings, and horns and thunder and horses and harps, the record seems to capture a piece of time, a piece of the past, to freeze a moment, or several moments, in amber, and in this way to make modern people more backward-looking and nostalgic. Every time you listen to a record, or a CD or MP3, you are in essence choosing to live in a pocket of the past.

From the beginning, musicians feared this new medium—a fear well portrayed in the Woody Allen movie *Sweet and Lowdown,* in which a Depression-era Jazz guitarist refuses to make a record, saying, "Once you record, everybody can steal your stuff. They steal your ideas. Why would you want to make something beautiful just to have some jerk copy it?" Before the Second World War, the Union of Working Musicians called a boycott on studio recording—they said it would cheat their members of concert dates. In competition with earlier versions of themselves, musicians feared they did not stand a chance. They were wrong, of course: the past can never replace the here-and-now of live music, especially Rock & Roll, when you are standing near the speaker. Records would only make people more hungry for the real thing.

Every new technology is quickly taken up by those who think they have found a new way to strike it rich. In the music business, these men ran the companies that grew out of the pioneering days. Thomas Edison's New York Phonograph, Victor Talking Machine, Columbia Gramophone, Electrical Musical Industries (EMI). These companies made records for the upper middle class, men and women who had the money and time to buy and listen to music. The producers preserved what seemed worth preserving: Chopin, Brahms, Beethoven. But in America, for everyone who seeks transcendence in high places, someone else searches low culture, the fugitive art of the poor. And so was born a new kind of record man, a figure who would have given Tom Edison hives, a slummer who spotted value in what was taken as the scrubbiest form of expression: farm and slave songs, ditties, dirges, hymns. Such record producers ditched the studio for the road, traveling by car, recording every cheap musician they happened across. This was done in the free-wheeling spirit of discovery: the spirit that drove John Hammond of Columbia

Records to discover and record Billie Holiday and Bob Dylan and Bruce Springsteen, to travel the country in a car fitted with a giant antenna; the spirit that Jerry Wexler felt when he heard Professor Longhair in the roadhouse in Algiers; the spirit Leonard Chess felt in the early sixties when he wandered the South recording in the fields. It's a romantic image: the white record man searching for the True Gen. And it goes back to one man, Alan Lomax, the ur-producer, who took Thomas Edison's invention and retargeted it from the opera house to the swamp.

Alan Lomax was born in Austin, Texas. He spent semesters at Harvard and Columbia, then went traveling, touring in an old coupe, a car that should be set alongside Lady Liberty out in the Harbor, a great holy arc that, on a few dozen reels of tape, carried the heritage of the Mississippi Delta, an area now awash in Wal-Marts and Kmarts and Targets, stores that choke off all things regionally strange. Lomax was an archivist, an art he learned from his father, John Lomax. During the Depression, father and son traveled to fishermen's shacks, prisons, work farms. At Angola State Penitentiary in Louisiana, they came across Huddie Ledbetter, the famous Leadbelly, who, with their help, recorded a body of work that plays like a creepy echo of old Jonah: "Goodnight Irene," "Midnight Special," "Rock Island Line."

Lomax hunted the low-down and authentic, music that casts out the demons. Speaking to a newspaper reporter about his visits to prison farms, his words could stand as mantra for the Rock-era record man: "The prisoners had dynamite in their performances. There was more emotional heat, more power, more nobility in what they did than all the Beethovens and Bachs could produce."

Lomax recorded talk by Jelly Roll Morton and Woody Guthrie, and songs by guitar players and singers. For the WPA, he released a series of records called Folkways, which, for the artists of the 1950s and 1960s, served as a crib sheet. Bob Dylan called Lomax "a missionary."

Lomax said his goal was a kind of "cultural equality." He wanted every society to have its art taken seriously. "It is the voiceless people of the planet who really have in their memories the ninety thousand years of human wisdom," he said. "I've devoted my life to an obsessive collecting of the evidence." It was a philosophy that set him apart from producers at the major record labels. He was the first true independent, working the fringes—a model followed by Leonard Chess and Ahmet Ertegun and Jimmy Iovine and Russell Simmons. Lomax believed that, by recording folk musicians and then letting these men and women hear themselves on tape, he could convince them of their worth. "When you play this material back, it changes everything," he said. "All at once, these poor ignorant players see that their music is just as good as anybody else."

By the 1940s, the music business had shaken itself out into what we recognize as the modern record industry, a world dominated by a handful of companies that, like the movie studios in Hollywood, are big enough and strong enough to dominate the entire market. Over the years, these companies came to control their industry in the manner of the five families of organized crime. If an independent record man or the leader of a Rock & Roll band wants to get his songs to the public, he at some point must work with one of these big companies. Even if his song is recorded by an independent, a big company will likely be involved in the release or the distribution: in this way, Big Paulie gets his cut. Buy-outs and failed gambles swell and trim their ranks, but they've generally been known as "The Majors." The Warner Music Group, perhaps the largest of the companies, is actually a confederacy of three distinct labels—Warner Brothers Music, Atlantic Records, and Elektra Records. EMI is the company created by the merger, in the 1930s, of Columbia Gramophone, the Gramophone Company, and Parlophone. Sony is Columbia under Japanese ownership. The Universal Music Group is Polygram plus MCA, a massive vacuum that has sucked up leagues of great independents: Mercury, Island, A&M, Motown, Def Jam. BMG, part of the German conglomerate Bertelsmann, is what remains of RCA Victor.

There are new majors and old majors, and now and then one falls out, which begs the question: What makes a record company a major label? It's like asking what makes a nation a global power: it comes down to a series of tangibles and intangibles, ways in which, through the soft power of marketing and the hard power of lawsuits, a record company can project force. But mostly, it's the ability of a company to control every aspect of a record's life, production to sale. Like an army or an empire, a major label is organized vertically—as opposed to an independent label, which might consist of just a few scouts gathered around a shtarker with a bankroll and a Rolodex. A major has the means to handle every step in the process: scouts to haunt the bars looking for and signing talent; lawyers to write up those deals, and other lawyers to handle the lawsuits that inevitably result from those write-ups; A&R (artist and repertoire) men to work with talent, readying them to record and tour; studios where the bands can cut the records; producers and engineers to direct the sessions; factories where CDs are pressed and packaged; truckers and pilots to haul the CDs around the world; distributors to put the CDs in the stores; managers to collect from the big chains—which harkens back to the three rules of the old-time independent: *pay me, pay me, fuck you, pay me.*

The president of a major acts less like a Lomax-style aficionado than like the desk-bound general of a vast army. He is a man who has been promoted right out of the fight, out of the clubs and the studios where he demonstrated the skills that got him promoted, and now finds himself operating in a white-collar world of board meetings and department heads and red tape and budgets. From here, the actual ground war of the business is as abstract as the splotchy paintings in the lobby. In a film, you would see such men as two-dimensional cutouts, shadows against a screen, the meaningless Charlie Brown rumble of adult voices. After years of expense accounts, these men find themselves remade as businessmen. If they were ever good record men, this new job is one for which they are ill suited. The seat-of-the-pants style of their early days only devalues stock price. They have lost the all-important freedom to fail. They have been turned into bureaucrats.

Of course, the bureaucracy conquered the world. When it's well run, it's a marvel, a humming machine of flowcharts and memos, a smooth progression up the ranks and out the door. As Albert Brooks says in *Lost in America*, "It's the carrot and the stick and the watch when you're seventy." It's the system that enabled the majors to make billions, to sell their stars across the world. Yet it has the fatal flaw of all bureaucracies. In certain moments, especially moments of rapid change, the majors are simply too big. They are slow-footed and lumbering and too careful because they have too much to lose. When a new thing comes along, they are always looking in the wrong direction. From their offices in the sky, major label execs cannot hear the street corner hip-hop, or hear it and are revolted, or hear it and think, *But where is the profit? Who's gonna buy this stuff?* In those rare cases when they do hear it, and get it, they worry about shareholders and board members who might be embarrassed by some greaseball shaking his hips on Ed Sullivan, or a gangbanger rapping about killing cops. Yes, a major can break a record or sell a hit, but it can never lead the way. With the birth of any new sound, dozens of independent labels, with names like Sun and Sub-Pop, appear like mushrooms after a storm. Black marketeers—they meet a need not filled by the mainstream. One such moment, the most explosive in the history of American music, came after the Second World War, with the country shaking off the green meanies that had dogged it since the Depression. It was the big American moment: a moment for entrepreneurs and sharks. The majors were deaf to this moment, because it was new and dangerous and fun, but to immigrant hustlers like Leonard Chess it was a fortune waiting to be made. And so rose a new generation of tycoon—the independent record man.

They were street-corner boys, sons of immigrants or immigrants themselves, the brother who did not go to college, the kid with the head for business; terrific talkers, torrents and cataracts and waterfalls of speech meant less to explain or clarify than to convince or prod or persuade or trick into signing. Hustlers and shysters and great imaginative schemers, forever on the verge of the big break, the golden moment, sometimes rich, sometimes poor, and who can tell the difference? They lived with their parents, then in dank, one-bedroom bachelor pads behind a tavern, then on the Island, in spooky Levittowns in dead first marriages they could not wait to escape. They loved the music they heard in the Negro dives a few blocks the wrong direction from the walkups where their cousins lived. Sometimes they loved it in the soaring heart-pumping way music should be loved and sometimes for what they could do with it. They wore suits stitched by Murray the Tailor or Joey the Jew. They hit the scene with all the pent-up energy of immigrant America, glad to get in the game, check in at the scorer's table, tear off their sweats, race onto the floor. They were tall and short, eyes blue or green, and some with eyes so dark no light reflected, long hair thrown over their ears, or else barbershop haircuts, hot-towel and newspaper and *Do me a favor, don't talk, just cut my fucking hair.* A generation that came of age in the fifties, jet-age businessmen who would invent the term "creative executive," who would blow their minds in the great smorgasbord of the sixties, would go from Roslyn or Merrick to sunny L.A. where rock stars would slip acid into their drinks and leave them shaking and whimpering and staring into a mirror as if searching for their own names.

Why did these men go into the record business? Because what else could an ambitious young Jew do that was half as exciting?

The colleges had thrown up a wall of quotas, and the white shoe firms weren't hiring, but there was music in the ghetto, fresh and raw and exciting, and it was all off the radar: the majors would not touch it. Turned away by Waspy companies, these legions of Sammy Glicks went ahead and built an industry of their own, the world of the independent record labels, companies geared to the low rumble of the Negro street: because they believed there was money in it, because they liked the music, because it was fun, because no one could shut them out, because chicks, chicks, chicks, because make your own hours, because it's better than selling schmatas, because if you want something build it, and also because, as immigrants with a personal knowledge of perse-cution, they were maybe the only Americans willing to form a partnership with poor blacks. These were the years when blacks and Jews found each other.

There were dozens of independent record men working in big cities in the Northeast and Midwest, Detroit, New York, Cleveland, wherever large immigrant populations were thrown together with blacks from the South—rural people reeling in the strange industrial landscape. In this sense, modern blues is trav-eling music, songs you sing when you are far from home, music of the Great Migration. ("When it gets late in the evening, I feel like going home," Muddy Waters sings. "When I woke up this morning, all I had was gone.") The record men rented offices on the edge of the slums, DMZs where Jewish and Italian neigh-borhoods ran into the ghetto. A few rooms in a tenement, a win-dow looking out on warehouses, drowsy shops, dirty river. Roulette, Jubilee, King. The most desperate operated as nomads, what the writer A. J. Leibling called Telephone Booth Indians. As their office phone, they gave out the number of a pay phone in the lobby of a building downtown and would camp in front of the phone for hours. A girl was hired to answer calls: "Hi Class Records!" And she shuffles some papers and hands the phone over to a sweating Telephone Booth Indian. "Kaplinsky here. And make it quick. It's my busy time."

Some of these independent record men got themselves mixed up with gangsters. Much has been made of such sinister underworld connections, but in fact old-time record men went to the shylocks only because they couldn't go to the banks. First Boston would simply not loan some immigrant sheeny ten grand to record a Negro from Alabama. But the gonifs were always ready with a roll. That's what the mob does: loan capital to those without options. A few grand on a twelve-point vig against the collateral of serious pain, or the company itself. Many labels paid off these loans, the details fading into colorful rumor. Others defaulted, and so the heavies found themselves in charge of a label—office, desks, cabinet full of contracts.

Joe Smith, the former president of Warner Brothers Music, a dapper, tanned Sinatra-like man, told me (on the deck of the Mondrian Hotel in Los Angeles) about acquiring Van Morrison's contract, "I bought it from mobsters. That's right! Mobsters! Van was with a company that was distributed by Atlantic. Its owner died and the label went into shambles. Nobody got paid. So I look through the wreckage and what do I find? Van Morrison. And I know I gotta get him. I just loved that voice! Then I find out the label has been financed by mob guys. Mob guys! In fact, they held Van's contract. It was their money. So there was a friend of mine, Joe Scandori, who managed Don Rickles, and Scandori had a club out on Long Island called the Eleganty. I said, 'Joe, find out how I can get to somebody who can sell me this contract.' So Joey comes back and says—and I'll never forget this—'these guys don't know what the hell they got, but they know you want it, whatever it is, so it's gonna cost you twenty-thousand dollars. And you gotta meet 'em at a warehouse on 9th Avenue in New York.' I had to finagle the books at Warners to get all that money in cash. They didn't want checks. Going up the stairs at the warehouse was a scene from a Scorsese movie. There's this building of a guy sitting there, and this other tall thin guy. Both of them are wearing hats.

" 'Joe Smith?'

" 'Yeah.'

" 'You got the money?'

" 'I got the money. You got the contract?'

" 'Yeah.'

" 'Who's signing?'

" 'I'm signing.'

" 'You authorized to sign?'

" 'Am I what?'

"I was afraid they would give me the contract, I would give them the money, then someone would whack me on the head and take back the contract. So I signed and ran. I jumped from the third floor down to the second floor landing and rolled. I know how to do that. I was a paratrooper. Then I ran out onto 9th Avenue and grabbed a cab."

The independent record men gave their labels names they thought sounded powerful, vibrant, American: Revolution. Modern. Excelsior. Ahmet Ertegun started Atlantic with cash borrowed from his dentist. His office was in Manhattan, a cramped room that doubled as a studio. Ertegun wrote lyrics to many of his label's early songs, including "Mess Around," by Ray Charles. It was cheaper to write a fake standard than to pay royalties for the real thing. "Play something lowdown from the whorehouses," Ertegun told Charles, who was sitting at the piano. In a high, reedy voice, Ertegun then sang:

Now you see that girl, with the diamond ring
She knows how to shake that thing
Mess around!
I declare, she can mess around
Ah, mess around
Everybody do the mess around!

Ertegun has this session on tape, which he played for me with tremendous satisfaction, saying, "And so that's how it was done."

Morris Levy, at Roulette, was a would-be mobster who ran with actual mobsters. He produced Jimmie Rogers and Ronnie Hawkins, and cut his clients to the bone. When he died, he was awaiting sentencing on an extortion conviction.

And there was the macher back east who was able on a bet to get a song on the charts, a song that did not exist, a feat that caused mild panic among the diner boys. *Jeeze, guys go to jail for doing stuff like that.* And there was Syd Nathan at King Records in Cincinnati, and Herb Abramson at Jubilee in New York (later a partner at Atlantic), and Lew Chudd at Imperial in Hollywood, and Bobby Robinson at Enjoy in Harlem, and Don Robey at Peacock in Houston, and the Schwartz brothers at Laurie in New York, and Herman Lubinsky at Savoy in Newark. And there was George Goldner, known as "The Oracle," at Rama Records in New York, who could stand before a row of blasting turntables and pick out the winner, saying, "Shit, shit, shit, *hit,* shit, shit."

But Chicago was the greatest of all music towns. It was a city on the make, a town with change in its pocket, a man with an afternoon to kill, and afternoon stretches into evening. The ghetto was dotted with record companies: Vee Jay, Robin, National. The founders of these labels were out each night in the dives, chasing the faintest shadow of an act. The best singers recorded for various companies, each time signing as if for the first time, recording some new version of the same old tune, collecting the usual fee—around fifty bucks. Because these musicians guaranteed exclusivity, they worked, in the manner of confidence men, under aliases—phony riverboat names. To compile the early songs of John Lee Hooker, you would have to look up releases by John Lee Hooker, but also by Delta John, John Williams, Birmingham Sam, Texas Slim. The fake names fooled no one and infuriated the label heads. In other words, the singers were ripping off the record men just as they were themselves getting ripped off. The record men were just better at it.

In Chicago, the market for race music had long been dominated by Bluebird Records, which was part of RCA Victor. During the war, Bluebird released sides by Lonnie Johnson, Big Bill

Broonzy, Tampa Red. Over time, because it faced little competition, the music on the label froze into a kind of house style, a collection of tricks and mannerisms. The Bluebird beat—the Soviet realism of race records, a synthetic approximation, music that relates to the real thing as a steak at the Sizzler relates to a steak at Peter Lugar's. It was in part a reaction to this dead sound that the Chicago scene exploded—it was a revolution, the toppling of an old order.

One of the new companies was called Aristocrat, a boutique label owned by Charles and Evelyn Aron, a husband-and-wife team that ran their business in the way of hobbyists: these were the sort of grit-seeking white Americans who fetishize all things black, products of the moment that produced Norman Mailer's essay, "The White Negro," which urged whitey to do like the black man and *live for today!* It was bullshit, of course, a projection onto a black community that, God knows, had enough to carry. It turned real people into a symbol: the Authentic Negro, the Soul Man. A special brand of bullshit that even now drives suburbanites to romanticize the bleakest of poverty. In a recent interview, Mick Jagger spoke of his own youthful fascination with black Blues singers. "We all wanted to live the life of Sonny Boy Williamson or Little Walter, but it was only because we did not really have to, because if you knew the actual details of that life, it was not very nice—being poor and sick and not getting paid and at the end of it all, dying young."

Evelyn Aron went to race music the way a cow goes to a salt lick: naturally and compulsively. It fed her deficiency, filled the void left by the white noise of America. It was this appetite that

gave her tremendous skill as a producer: she had the ability to
hear the music for what it was and not measure it against tradi-
tional music or jazz or what had gone before. Leonard, who grew
up alongside the ghetto, had no such romantic notions. As a
result, he tended to operate with too much brain: *What is it? Has
something like it worked in the past?*

Charles Aron, in this narrative, anyway, because I am sure he
was very real to those who loved him or were annoyed by him, figures mostly by his absence. It was Evelyn Aron who recruited the
artists and produced the records—in studios rented from the
majors. In 1948, when Leonard approached Evelyn Aron to form a
partnership, she was hesitant. She knew Leonard from the
Macomba, and from the scene, and it wasn't that she absolutely
could not stand Leonard, it was just that, well, you know, Evelyn
came from one of these assimilated Jewish families, and she was
proper and well raised, and here comes this grasping, striving, big-
nosed Jew from Poland. She must have looked at him the way the
German Jews looked at the Easterners who came off the boat with
their prayer books and side curls—ok, maybe that's going a bit far,
but Jews like Evelyn have always been especially bugged by Jewy
Jews like Leonard, who might blow their cover. But Leonard had
something to offer, which was an inside on the scene, a pass to
the salt lick. He had already locked up Andrew Tibbs, who every
producer in town wanted to record. In return, Leonard wanted a
job; he wanted Evelyn to teach him the record business.

The deal was struck in 1948. Within weeks, Leonard was splitting time between the Macomba and his new job. (For the most
part, Phil was left to run the bar.) Leonard brought Sammy Goldberg

with him to Aristocrat, the scout who first turned him on to Andrew Tibbs. Goldberg and Chess would become a powerful team. Together they would fill the roster of Aristocrat. Funny. You would think black singers would have flocked to the salt-lick love of Evelyn Aron, when, in fact, it mostly flipped them out. The grasping, striving, eager, pushy, greedy, hungry, vulgar, loud, demanding, gruff business sense of Leonard—that's what they wanted. He was like one of those no-frills old cars that backfires and belches but it gets you there. And yes, it's funny, how this Polish immigrant, this kid who did not even learn English until he was in school, winds up at a company called Aristocrat. But that's America: no past, no pedigree, the great ones give birth to themselves.

LEONARD HAD FOUND his calling—no more gun toting, no more stumble-down drunks, no more drug flushing. The Macomba was left to fade into the distance, a butte in a Western. Leonard would now meet the world from behind a desk, like a businessman. It's easy to see why so many young hustlers were finding their way into race music—it was brand new, for one thing, these guys were making up their own rules. And the setup was beautiful. Overhead was nothing. Twenty, thirty bucks for rent, some chairs, a secretary, gas money. The musicians were paid only when they were recording and then it was scale: $41.25 for a three-hour session. Can you believe it? And many of the early records were just one guy on a piano or guitar. A license from the musician's union might cost another twenty bucks, and studio time rented at anywhere from twenty-five to forty bucks an hour, and throw in a few hundred for pressing, and for three or four hundred dollars you've got a record.

In the early years, Leonard distributed himself, loading records into the trunk of his sedan, Cadillac being the preferred ride of all self-respecting record men. If a record flopped, Leonard was out a few weeks work and some C-notes. But if it hit, he might gross fifty, sixty grand; if it really hit, he might gross a hundred K—2 or 3 percent of that went to the artist in royalties (the majors paid closer to 5 percent), but the rest, depending on how honest he was with the government, was profit. From an initial layout of two or three hundred dollars, a record man could bring in a thousand dollars. And that was before he hit the real big time.

To record Tibbs, Leonard rented a studio at Columbia Records. He didn't go in there like some timid novice but with tremendous confidence: men of his particular vintage tended to believe that everyone is pretending anyway, so if you just feigned knowledge, the real thing was sure to follow. As a result, Leonard was one of those producers who is always shouting and cutting in on the speaker, calling for another take, banging a table, saying, *Come on, boys, sing it like if you don't make this girl you're gonna die!* "It's the same way movie directors work," Marshall Chess told me. "Pulling the best performance out of all the players. Remember, those records were made on two tracks, so there weren't overdubs like now, when they use forty-eight tracks. You can't keep doing it a hundred times. The secret was getting the best performance out of the whole band: fuck it up and you can't use it."

At one session, when Leonard didn't like what the drummer

Phil Chess in the studio with the Muddy Waters Band. Muddy, left, tunes his guitar as Little Walter plays the harp. Phil, looking like a Belushi, calls for the check. (BMI/Michael Ochs Archives.com)

was laying down—*the schmuck just couldn't nail it*—Leonard shouts, "Step aside, motherfucker, let me show you how it's done," slides behind the kit, calls time, and starts banging. You can still hear it on the classic, "She Moves Me," Muddy Waters shouting—

> *She moves me when she gets drunk*
> *Says I'm not nowhere*
> *Call me a dumb bear*
> *Moves me*
> *And I don't see how it's done*

Got a pocket full of money
Don't give me none

—as Leonard hammers away, laying down the backbeat that would become the pulse of Rock & Roll. "All my dad's knowledge came out of the bar," Marshall said. "The big labels would send A&R kids to hang around clubs for a few hours, and then they were supposed to know about music, but my father lived in those clubs. And he knew the one big thing: You got to give the street what the street wants."

"Leonard worked real hard in the studio," said Jimmy Rogers, one of the great Chess guitarists. "We would get in there in the afternoon, and he wouldn't let us out until two, three in the morning."

"A lot of times Chess would be telling the artist how to sing and we'd throw him out his own studio," said Willie Dixon, who became one of the great songwriters and producers at the label. "We'd say, 'Get the fuck out of here, Leonard.' He would be in there shooting the bull, starting arguments and calling guys names: 'Hey, you son of a son. Can't you get it right?' He did it to boost morale, to get us fighting, cussing back. He figured he could tantalize the musicians, get them upset and they would use that upset in the song."

The Tibbs record is a cautionary tale—it shows how everything can go wrong. A few thousand were pressed. Side A was "Union Blues," a song about the life of a union man, a flat song to everyone but the Teamsters, truckers, and box handlers, who found it offensive, and so—or so the story goes—refused to ship it, letting the records pile up in the warehouses. Side B was "Bilbo Is Dead," an attack on segregationist Senator Theodore Bilbo, who had just died. In those parts of the South where the Teamsters let the record through, it was smashed by angry white mobs. So started Leonard Chess in the music business: he sent his record out into the whirlwind—and these things are really no more than totems of the people who make them—and it came back smashed up, and spat upon, and undelivered.

For his next release, Leonard stayed close to home, recording Tommy Archia, leader of the Macomba house band. Leonard and Phil stayed up all night packing records, hiring a neighborhood kid to help.

Tommy Lipuma, who headed Verve Records, started in the business in the fifties working for a man much like Leonard. One morning, this boss watched Lipuma, just nineteen, pack records, sleeves and discs scattered across the floor.

The boss said, "Hey, kid, you got any change?"

Lipuma took seventy-two cents out of his pocket.

"Hand it over," said the boss.

Lipuma handed it over and the boss chucked the money at the wall.

"Do you like what I just did to your money?"

"No, sir."

The boss pointed at the records and said, "And I don't like what you're doing to my money. Treat the product with a little fucking respect."

"Those first-generation guys were bandits," Joe Smith told me. "They were bandits because it was their own money. It wasn't like some executive playing with a corporate payroll. For Leonard Chess, every dime was in those records. If it hits, he's rich. If it flops, he's busted. So he was out there hustling."

Leonard loaded a few thousand Archia records into his Cadillac and set off across the country. Aristocrat had no distribution, which meant Leonard had to hand-sell to local distributors, who worked freelance, taking on only those records they thought would make it. In Pittsburgh, after hours on the road, Leonard met with the distributor for Mercury. He said he would take the Archia record only after some demonstration of its worth. Leonard and the distributor got in the car and went looking for a store where they could try to sell the record. Leonard would not stop until they reached the dilapidated streets of the ghetto. They went into a drugstore. The owner came out front.

Do you carry records?

On occasion.

Leonard dropped the record onto a turntable. And there was Tommy Archia blasting away, a racy piece of Chicago rising up like a magic lantern. When the record ended, the man said, "You got a real hit there." The distributor said he would take a hundred copies—OK, not a runaway Britney Spears–type deal, but a start. And with each new record, Leonard built on it, a few more distributors, a few more sales. But even then, he must have known something was missing, some seal had not been broken; he was still slogging in the Bluebird beat. He was still looking for the new thing, the fresh sound that would carry him to the big time. And it was looking for him, too.

3

They Call It the Blues, but It Makes You Want to Dance

The first Blues record was released in the early 1920s. "Crazy Blues" by Mamie Smith. The music itself had been around much longer. Some believe the Blues are no less than the remnant of the ancient drum heavy-music the slaves brought from Africa—the relic that remained when their clothes, language, religion, history, and mythology had been stripped away. "All blues songs come from the original tom toms of Africa," Willie Dixon writes in his autobiography. "That's the reason I say, the blues are the roots and other musics are the fruits." I like this little rhyme, but I think it's mostly not true. If an old African music does survive in the Blues, it's less as a presence than as an absence—a longing for what's been lost. The Blues, which must've sounded so foreign and otherworldly to its first white audiences— hence the need to tie it to Africa—is a purely American invention: like organized crime and baseball, it's homegrown but so exotic there is an urge to surround it with a fanciful history of mystical origins: *It comes from the black hand of Sicily, it comes from a game played by the Aztecs, it comes from the Tom Toms of Africa.* The Blues probably do contain some fragment of an older culture, but it is a fragment that has been so crossbred with the sound of modern America, the result is something utterly new.

The Blues were born in the years after the Civil War, born and raised, like most of its practitioners, beyond the gaze of the mainstream, and so this birth remains something of a mystery. Some say the big moment came in New Orleans in the 1800s, when, as a backlash to Reconstruction, the white aristocracy enacted the strict racial laws that drove thousands of mulattos, some of the best-trained musicians in the city, from their perch in white society to the rundown precincts of the French Quarter, to the dives and whorehouses, where the formal music came to mix with the rougher music of the freed slaves, resulting in a weird hybrid that would later be made famous by Jelly Roll Morton and Louis Armstrong. During World War I, when the police, at the request of the U.S. Navy, who were losing more and more men to the clap, shut down Storyville, the city's red-light district, where most of this new music was performed, the musicians wandered away—a diaspora of players who scattered the sound across the South. It would continue north, picking up the sound of each town and plantation until, in Chicago, it took on the rattle of the metropolis, but it never lost the low-down mood of the whorehouses, the grind you still hear in the best of Rock & Roll.

By the turn of the century, various regional styles of the Blues developed. There was the bone-dry style of West Texas, Blind Lemon Jefferson and Lightnin' Hopkins; the sophisticated style of Big Joe Turner and Kansas City; the spooky primitive style of

the Sea Islands in Georgia. But the Blues that made the trip
north to Chicago and so, in the Darwinian sense, was fated to
survive, to pass on its DNA to Rock & Roll, was the Blues of the
Mississippi Delta. The Delta, in case you are wondering, is the
sweep of fertile floodplain that runs like a green-backed snake
along the Mississippi. It covers parts of Mississippi and Alabama
and Louisiana. It is also a suggestion of class or style, so it is
defined more narrowly depending on whom you ask. A rich white
farmer might tell you the Delta is everything south of the Peabody
Hotel in Memphis. A professor of history might tell you it is those
towns on the bluffs high above the river that were seiged during
the Civil War. But those interested in American music will tell
you the Delta is that humid, rolling, buggy country where the
Yazoo River meets the Mississippi—a country where everything
faces either south to New Orleans and the past, or north to
Chicago and the future. Aficionados have come to regard it as a
primal landscape, a troubled Eden. The roads that cross it—
roads that the first practitioners escaped along and felt hemmed
in by—have become as symbolic as the Tigris and Euphrates.
Highway 61, Highway 51, Highway 49—they turn up in song
after song, first as a recollection of a place, then as a recollection
of a recollection, a shift, from real life to pose, that marks the
end of the vibrant period in any art. On his records *Highway 51*
and *Highway 61 Revisited,* Bob Dylan shouts out the names of
these roads as if they were a spell, words that can call forth the
power of a tradition.

   This music made its historical appearance in 1903—a mystical encounter that has been written about and discussed until

it's become a legend. W. C. Handy, the leader of the most accomplished Negro band of the time, was waiting for a train in Tutwiler, Mississippi. It was a soupy Delta night, the bugs swinging their sharp little hammers, the fields rolling away. Handy had started to drift but was awoken by a man in ragged clothes. He carried a guitar. He sat across from Handy and started to play. The song had one lyric, and the man sang it again and again: "Goin where the Southern cross the dog, goin where the Southern cross the dog"—reference to that place where the Yazoo & Mississippi Valley Railroad, the Yellow Dog, cut across the tracks of the Illinois Central on their way to Chicago. Handy later spoke of how startled he was by this music. By holding a knife across the guitar strings, the man slurred the chords into a moan that seemed to approximate a human voice: the guitar was talking. This was the first known appearance of what came to be known as Delta Blues. As a result, much curiosity surrounds the encounter: if the Delta is the troubled Eden—*just let me have it*—this man is its Adam, the common ancestor, the father of every bluesman and rock & roller. He appears on the platform just long enough to sing his song and then vanishes into the night, or maybe it is Handy who is gone, away on the train, looking out at the rolling countryside, the chill in his bones, the lyric winding through his mind. *Goin where the Southern cross the dog.*

The father of Delta Blues, the man who went into the studio and cut the first sides, did not appear for another twenty years. If this were a bible story, as probably it should be, this passage of time would be marked by the ebb and flow of rivers. His name was Charley Patton. He was a drifter and a gambler who hung around the Dockery Plantation, a few thousand acres on the Sunflower River. Because Patton played there, and because so many singers worked in its fields, the plantation is considered the home of the Delta Blues. It's where the shouts first went from the fields into the juke joints. In the years just after World War I, Patton, by setting these shouts to guitar and building them into a coherent structure, remade them into country Blues. In photos, Patton is a light-skinned black man, jug-eared, funny looking, a guitar in his lap. He played in roadhouses across the South, where his songs were marveled at and copied. By 1929, his following was big enough to convince a local (white) merchant to fund a recording session: he sent Patton to Richmond, Indiana, and later to Appleton, Wisconsin, where he drank whiskey, stumbled, cursed, and cut the dozen or so sides that stand as the headwater of the Blues. "One of These Days I'll Be Gone," "Hang It on the Wall," "Some Summer Day," songs that would be performed and recorded again and again—different lyrics but the same tune, the same lyrics but different tune, or the same lyrics *and* the same tune but in a different style. Sometimes there was just enough variation to keep a performer out of the courts.

Most of Patton's songs carry echoes of even earlier songs. He was something of an archeologist, or a magpie, piecing together art from noise found drifting across the Delta. It's a tradition, appropriation and reappropriation, that explains the persistent recurrence of lyrics, phrases that appear in song after song, until the original meaning has faded like the face of an old statue. Even when the original meaning is lost, the lyrics linger as an invocation, a connection to the primitive power of the man W. C. Handy heard in Tutwiler. Here is Robert Palmer explaining the practice in his book *Deep Blues*:

> Most and quite possibly all of these phrases were unoriginal. They were floating formulas, some of which came from older ballads and spirituals while others were folk sayings from everyday figures of speech. Phrases like, "I'm going up the country" or "You've got to reap just what you sow" were repeated by countless wandering songsters throughout the latter half of the nineteenth century and probably figured in black music before emancipation.

The phrases which Patton preserved would continue into the modern era, where they turn up in pop songs the way Latin turns up in American speech. At some point, every self-respecting rocker sings about *reaping just what you sow*, or *going up the country*, or *going down the line*—references often made by singers from places like Liverpool or Leeds who probably don't much know or care what they mean.

Charley Patton seems, in his songs, anyway, and probably walking around too, to dwell in a world halfway between the juke joint and the church. Now and then, in the middle of a tune, he stumbles out of a lyric into a sermon—"*Well, friends, I want to tell you, tell you, when He comes down his hair will be like lamb's wool, and his eyes like flames of fire, and every man is gonna know that He is the living God, and around his shoulder-bone be a rainbow, and his head be like fine bread, and my friends, I want you to*

*know again that He says we gonna have clear water flowing through
the garden, water clear as a preacher, and the wind can't blow on
you no more, and the dogs don't bite"*—then kicks back into the
groove.

Patton was not the first blues singer, but he was the first poor
blues singers on record, so with him we get the first thrilling
sense of this music as a kind of oral history, a collection of inci-
dents and happenings and conquests, a calypso passed on and
preserved. There were newspapers in Jackson, Mississippi, and
Natchez and Vicksburg, of course, but this music told another
story: it was a counternarrative, a secret language, an underground current of images pieced together from the oldest rumors,
a ghost train running beyond the Yellow Dog, a history of all-
night gamblers and drifters and killers and con men. Like most
of literature, it consists of just a few stories told again and again:
A man walks into a bar, there is a card game, a knife fight. Consider
"Stagger Lee," a song that has probably been performed by more
artists in more styles than any other folk song in history. It's been
recorded as "Stagolee," "Stag-O-Lee," "Stackolee," "Stack-A-Lee,"
"Stagerlee," with each singer taking his stab at the narrative the
way, during the Renaissance, each painter took his stab at George
and the Dragon, or the way, in Hollywood, each director takes
his stab at the Shoot-out at the OK Corral.

The song can be traced back to an actual murder that, in 1895,
made the St. Louis newspaper:

THE GLOBE DEMOCRAT (December 28, 1895): William Lyons,
25, a levee hand, was shot in the abdomen yesterday evening

at 10 o'clock in the saloon of Bill Curtis, at Eleventh and Morgan Streets, by Lee Sheldon, a carriage driver. Lyons and Sheldon were friends and were talking together. Both parties, it seems, had been drinking and were feeling in exuberant spirits. The discussion drifted to politics, and an argument was started, the conclusion of which was that Lyons snatched Sheldon's hat from his head. The latter indignantly demanded its return. Lyons refused, and Sheldon withdrew his revolver and shot Lyons in the abdomen. When his victim fell to the floor Sheldon took his hat from the hand of the wounded man and coolly walked away. He was subsequently arrested and locked up at the Chestnut Street Station. Lyons was taken to the Dispensary, where his wounds were pronounced serious. Lee Sheldon is also known as "Stag" Lee.

The incident appeared in song a short time later, and so began its trip into the repertoire of dozens of musicians. By the time it appeared in the mainstream, it had been cleaned up and made ready for telling, as if it had been run through the typewriter of a script doctor. Here's the version Lloyd Price made into a Rock & Roll hit in 1959:

I was standin' on the corner
When I heard my bull dog bark
He was barkin' at the two men
Who were gamblin' in the dark

It was Stagger Lee and Billy
Two men who gambled late

Stagger Lee threw a seven
Billy swore that he threw eight

"Stagger Lee," said Billy
"I can't let you go with that
"You have won all my money
And my brand-new Stetson hat"

Stagger Lee went home
And he got his .44
He said, "I'm goin' to the ballroom
"Just to pay that debt I owe"

Stagger Lee went to the ballroom
And he strolled across the ballroom floor
He said "You did me wrong, Billy"
And he pulled his .44

"Stagger Lee," said Billy
"Oh, please don't take my life!
I've got three hungry children
And a very sickly wife"

Stagger Lee shot Billy
Oh, he shot that poor boy so bad
That a bullet went through Billy
And broke the bartender's glass

Versions of this song have been recorded by dozens of musicians. As Folk: Bob Dylan, Pete Seeger, the Negro Prison Singers of the Mississippi State Penitentiary, David Bromberg (as "Mrs. DeLion's Lament"), Woody Guthrie, Tim Hardin, Dale Miller, Sparky Rucker, Dave Van Ronk, Logan English, Cisco Houston, Tom Rush. As Country: Mickey Giley, Charlie Pride, the Round Peak Band, Freddy Weller, the New Lost City Ramblers, Merle Travis, Ed Haley & Bob Wills. As Bluegrass: Doc and Merle Watson, Tim and Molly O'Brien. As Rhythm & Blues: Furry Lewis (as "Billy Lyons and Stackalee"), Kansas Joe McCoy, Dr. John, Champion Jack Dupree, the Fabulous Thunderbirds, the Isley Brothers, Johnny Otis, Wilbert Harrison, Curtis Jones, Wilson Pickett, Professor Longhair, Taj Mahal, Dave Bartholomew, Mississippi John Hurt, Ma Rainey, Mickey Baker, Roy Book- binder, Honeyboy Edwards, Jesse Fuller, Ike and Tina Turner. As Jazz: Cab Calloway, Duke Ellington. As Hawaiian: Sol Ho'o'pi'i. As Rock & Roll: Nick Cave & the Bad Seeds, Dion & the Belmonts, Neil Diamond, Fats Domino, the Grateful Dead, Bill Haley and the Comets, Sleepy LaBeef, Jerry Lee Lewis, the McCoys, Terry Melcher, Sandy Nelson, P. J. Proby, the Righteous Brothers, Johnny Rivers, Tommy Roe, Sam the Sham and the Pharaohs, Neil Sedaka, Southside Johnny and the Asbury Jukes, Willie and the Poorboys, the Youngbloods, Huey Lewis and the News.

Each singer and group added to the song until it grew into an epic. Tracking the process you understand how the ancient Greek poems evolved in the years before they were put down on paper. By our time, renditions of "Stagger Lee" are mostly commentary, shock tactics, or deconstruction, anything to get back to the orig- inal thrill of the old tune.

The Grateful Dead:

1940, Christmas Eve, with the full moon over town
Stagger Lee shot Billy DeLyon, he blew that poor boy down
Do you know what he shot him for, what do you make of that
'Cause Billy DeLyon threw lucky dice
and won Stagger Lee's Stetson hat

Nick Cave & the Bad Seeds:

She saw the barkeep, said, "O God, he can't be dead!"
Stag said, "Well, just count the holes in the motherfucker's
head"
She said, "You ain't look like you scored in quite a time
Why not come to my pad? It won't cost you a dime"
Mr. Stagger Lee

"But there's something I have to say before you begin
You'll have to be gone before my man Billy Dilly comes in
Mr. Stagger Lee"

"I'll stay here till Billy comes in, till time comes to pass
And furthermore I'll fuck Billy in his motherfucking ass"
Said Stagger Lee

"I'm a bad motherfucker, don't you know
And I'll crawl over fifty good pussies
Just to get one fat boy's asshole"
Said Stagger Lee

Just then Billy Dilly rolls in and he says, "You must be
That bad motherfucker called Stagger Lee"
Stagger Lee

"Yeah, I'm Stagger Lee and you better get down on your knees
And suck my dick, because if you don't you're gonna be dead"
Said Stagger Lee

Billy dropped down and slobbered on his head
And Stag filled him full of lead

Stagger Lee is the history of the Blues in miniature—a secret language of poor blacks, discovered and co-opted and remade and packaged and sold and left for dead by whites. It is the story of Elvis Presley and Leonard Chess. It is the story of Nick Cave, who, trying to replicate the creepiness of the old music, can do no better than traffic in lascivious images. It is the story of Rock & Roll.

In the beginning, the songs were shocking in their mere existence—a voice of those thought to be voiceless. Most of the Blues served as a chronicle of local events, as did early versions of "Stagger Lee." But behind many of these songs was a single disaster, buried deep in the memory of the music: the flood of 1927, the worst in the history of the Mississippi. The levees burst, twenty thousand acres were washed away, six hundred thousand people were left without homes. The entire Delta was under water. It was the flood of Noah, a trauma that runs through the Blues like ribbon. Charley Patton sang about it in "High Water Everywhere":

The terrible Mississippi flood of 1927 that, in the book of the Blues, is like the awesome flood of Noah. (© Bettmann/Corbis)

> *So high the water was risin'*
> *Our men sinkin' down*
> *Man, the water risin'*
> *At places all around*
> *It was fifty men and children*
> *Come to sink and drown*

Does it reverberate? On his recent album, *Love and Theft*—and please consider the meaning of that title—Bob Dylan sings a new version of "High Water," which he dedicates to Charley Patton:

High water risin'
Six inches 'bove my head
Coffins droppin' in the street
Like balloons made out of lead
Water pourin' into Vicksburg
Don't know what I'm going to do
"Don't reach out for me," she said
"Can't you see I'm drowning too"

This tragedy was reported by the mainstream, of course, by the newspapermen and writers, specifically by William Faulkner, a Mississippi native, whose story "The Flood" offers a rare glimpse of the landscape of the Blues as seen from the other side of the racial divide:

The truck passed a Negro cabin. The water was up to the window ledges. A woman clutching two children squatted on a ridge pole, a man and half-grown youth, standing waist-deep, were hoisting a squealing pig onto the slanting roof of a barn.

The narrator notices a Negro musician. For a moment, it's as if Patton himself had wandered into the story:

The sound of the guitar had not stopped and now the convicts saw him—a young, black, lean-hipped man, the guitar slung by a piece of cotton line about his neck. He mounted the levee, still picking it. He carried nothing else, no food, no change of clothes, not even a coat.

Wherever Patton played, men in overalls or picking clothes stood along the stage, swaying and humming, their dark eyes bouncing like superballs, tracing each shrug and gesture. This was the next generation, men who would preserve and remake the Blues—*the founders never do make it to the promised land*—and carry it beyond Mississippi. One night, a group of these men, including Son House, a failed preacher and convicted killer (one of his failings as a preacher), who, when giving a definition of the Blues, said, fittingly, "That woman told me she loved me and now she gone and I'm gonna kill her—that's the blues," and Tommy Johnson, who invented many of the stage tricks, such as the duckwalk and the behind-the-back solo, that would later be taken up by Chuck Berry and Jimi Hendrix, were approached by a gawky kid named Robert Johnson. He was twenty. He had a simple face and wide-set eyes that, in pictures, are remote and dreamy. He was born in a shack in Hazelhurst, Mississippi. He was drawn to the wandering life of the working musician. He said he wanted these men to hear him play. They must have looked at him the way an older brother looks at a younger brother when, for the first time, the younger brother picks up the remote control.

Go ahead, said Son House.

In the mythology of Rock & Roll, this scene is on permanent display: Robert Johnson on a stool, tuning his guitar—*all right, I'm visualizing*—strumming a few chords and launching into a song, and it sounds like absolute shit. The kid cannot play a lick. The older men burst out laughing.

Then he is gone, one month, two months, three months—who's counting? The rains come, the rains go. The cattails grow, the cattails die. Son House is crossing the fields, the land swampy and strange in early evening, when he hears music blasting from a juke joint up on the levee. It is rollicking, haunted. He tops the rise, river rolling away in the night. The joint is jammed with people. He pushes inside. He can't believe it. It's the kid, Robert Johnson hammering away on guitar, fingers blurring like propellers, spinning into a void. He drives his heel into the floorboards, moans like a dog. He has the broken-off neck of a Coke bottle on his index finger and uses it as a slide, slurring and smearing the chords. Bottleneck guitar. His eyes grow wide and he shouts as if possessed. His eyelids droop and he whispers and cries. People said listening to Robert Johnson was like listening to a whole band. His music was the wine that spills over the rim of the glass, that extra bit of soul you cannot contain in your body. It was so new and so strange and yet still the Blues and so familiar. Robert Johnson had taken the music of Charley Patton and brought it to yield. Muddy Waters once watched him play from a distance. "It was Friar's Point," said Muddy. "And this guy had a lot of people around him. They said it was Robert. I peeked over, then I left. Because that was a dangerous man."

This wild burst of talent, this careening, careering appearance of the modern, led to rumors that have dogged the legacy of Robert Johnson ever since. When asked how he learned to play, so well and fast—*and where the hell have you been these last many months?*—Johnson did a sort of *aw shucks*–type deal, or else talked about a trip through the roadhouses, old-timers teaching him tricks, sitting by a hotel window in the night, fingering his guitar as the moon pours down. Some believed he had, in fact, cut a deal with the Devil—his soul for this wicked ability on guitar. Even the particulars were explained: Robert went to a crossroads in the country, in the middle of the great bowl of the Delta, no house or farm or light for miles. He stood there as the moon rose and fell, as the wind moved in the grass, as the stars tacked across the sky. An old man came up the road. He did not talk or ask Robert what he wanted. He simply took the guitar and tuned it and played a song and handed it back, and just like that, Robert Johnson had the gift, was a sort of hydrant, in fact; open the cover and the music pours out. His relatives claimed they knew the crossroads where the deal was made. "The devil came and gave Robert his talent and told him he had eight more years to live on this earth."

(In *this* book, Leonard Chess is, of course, the Devil, the Nosferatu-like businessman who plays a tune and hands back the guitar and then extracts his fee.)

Why the crossroads? Because that is where you make the choice: life or death, fallen or saved, this world or the next. In Mississippi, a land without hills or oceans, a flat land that leads on to further flatness, that, at night, is a study of black on black, the crossroads are the only landmarks—where here meets there and elsewhere becomes an actual prospect. The Blues, and its bastard son Rock & Roll, are therefore the music of the flats, and so it is fitting that the music would make its way to Chicago, a city where the only hills are ravines, holes in the ground. The crossroads is where Robert Johnson, and a whole generation of singers and songwriters and duckwalkers, chose the juke joint over the church. It is where Rock & Roll made the deal that bought it eternal life—*Rock & Roll will never die*—but that also made it forever the Devil's music. Like Lucifer, it is fallen from heaven, the founders having built those first songs out of choir hymns and spirituals, like dragging the church into the gutter, doing something behind the back of God. That's why many of the pioneers, like Son House, were failed preachers, or, like Little Richard and Solomon Burke and Al Green, went from pulpit to bandstand and back again—from "Wop bob a loo bop" to "Man is born of woman's womb."

To this day, every rock & roller lives under the contract Robert Johnson struck at the crossroads the way every American lives under the deal agreed to in Philadelphia in 1776. You hear it in the voodoo songs of Muddy Waters, or when Howlin' Wolf sings, "We gonna knock out all the windows, we gonna bust down all the doors"; in the songs of Judas Priest and Megadeath, in the songs of bands sued by parents who say they promote devil worship; or when Mick Jagger sings, "I was around when Jesus Christ had his moment of doubt and pain." It's a game that can get out of control, as at the Stones concert in Altamont, California, where the Hells Angels, hired as bodyguards, stabbed and killed a fan while Jagger sang "Sympathy for the Devil." The crossroads is where the Blues came into possession of the dark magic. It's mostly through drugs that musicians try to return to the crossroads: the crossroads is now the street corner where the junk is scored. By referring to Robert Johnson, such musicians claim a partnership in the old contract. In "2 Kool 2 Be 4-Gotten," Lucinda Williams sings:

No dope smoking
No beer sold after 12 o'clock
Rosedale, Mississippi
Magic City Juke Joint
Mr. Johnson sings over in a corner by the bar
Sold his soul to the devil so he can play guitar

Eric Clapton has made a career out of the crossroads, as in his cover of Johnson's own song on the subject:

I went down to the crossroads,
Tried to flag a ride,
Nobody seemed to know me,
Everybody passed me by.

Robert Johnson was relatively unknown in his own lifetime. He drifted beyond the radar, beyond notice of those who review and record, leaving a scatter of recollections that would be pored over by scholars. Part of his appeal comes from this mystery. Though he lived in modern times, we know less about him than about Emperor Hadrian. As a result, he is a perfect figure for aficionados. Unlike Muddy Waters, he never sued a publishing company; unlike Howlin' Wolf, he never appeared on a television variety show. He can stand for whatever you want him to stand for. Mostly, he was a creature of the road, wandering from town to town, playing at house parties and bars. He made it as far north as New York City, and wandered all over the South, a life he chronicled in songs like "Ramblin' on My Mind": "I got ramblin' on my mind, hate to leave my baby, you treat me so unkind." It was a lifestyle glorified and emulated by rock stars who tried to replicate the Robert Johnson experience without hassle and heartache—Bob Johnson with money. Whereas the bluesman might roll into town on the back of a pickup truck and play on a street corner, the Allman Brothers came in a fleet of air-conditioned coaches and played in arenas where thousands cheered as they sang their Robert Johnson–influenced, "Ramblin' Man," *trying to make a livin', doing the best they can.*

Johnson created the modern Blues song. Earlier songs had been a cobble of floating verses; Johnson turned this hodgepodge into a narrative. Over the course of five days in 1936 and 1937, in a studio in Texas, with the help of an engineer who later remembered him as a nice young man, Johnson recorded twenty-seven sides. In the way that Gershwin created the template for Jazz, melodies that could be remade by each new generation, these sides were to become the template of the Blues and of Rock & Roll. They are forever being rediscovered and marveled at and imitated. As all Russian literature is said to have come out from under Gogol's overcoat, all Rock & Roll can be said to have come out of the bottleneck of Robert Johnson.

By the 1940s, the legend had finally begun to reach white aficionados in the North, and so, in the summer of 1941, Alan Lomax came in search of Robert Johnson. When Lomax explained who he was looking for, he was met with blank stares. Someone finally said, *Yes, Robert played all around here, but that was years ago—Robert Johnson is dead.* It happened in 1938 in Greenwood, Mississippi. Johnson and Honeyboy Edwards had been offered a few dollars to play a house party in one of those crappy sheds that shudder and roll like a sloop in a storm. Johnson ran through his songs and dozens of Delta favorites and was throwing back shots and pretty soon was seriously drunk. He caught the eye of a woman—the wife of the host. Robert was a prolific ladies' man. He was flirting like mad. Someone handed him a whiskey. He drank it down. The cramps came right away, but he kept playing, carried by the music. In the early morning, drenched with sweat, he stumbled off the makeshift stage. The room reeled, faces sailed away. There was no money for a doctor. He was put to bed in a shack. He suffered for three weeks, then died. Johnny Shines, the great bluesman, said Robert Johnson spent his last minutes on earth crawling on his hands and knees and barking like a dog.

So no, Alan Lomax, you cannot record Robert Johnson, but if you gather your gear, we will take you to a young man who sounds just like Robert Johnson, plays in the same bottleneck style, sings in same eerie falsetto. His name is McKinley Morganfield, but everyone calls him Muddy Waters.

The Delta is a Mark Rothko painting: green strip of land, blue strip of sky, the sky so flawlessly blue it makes your eyes sting. The wind is hot and dusty and comes in low like a slider. Lomax is blasting down dirt roads, across the open country, to the Stovall Plantation, thousands of acres of cotton, men and women working in the rows, white barracks thrown across the spongy fields like dice. These people shop in the company store, drink in the company canteen, draw lines of credit their salaries will never catch. Muddy lives in a little wood house. At night, he can hear the Illinois Central. If the sound of a train whistle at night doesn't touch you, you probably can't be touched.

McKinley Morganfield was born in Rolling Fork, Mississippi, in 1913, in a house off Highway 61. He was raised in Clarksdale, Mississippi, by his grandmother. "When I got big enough to crawl, I would play in the mud and try to eat it," he told Robert Palmer in *Deep Blues*. "Grandma started that Muddy thing and after we got near Clarksdale the kids started the Waters." When he was seventeen, he built his first guitar, "out of a box and a stick for a neck. Couldn't do much with it, but that's how you learn." A few years later, he sold a mule for two bucks fifty and bought a Stella. He learned to play listening to the radio. He ordered his first grownup guitar from the Sears catalogue—an eleven-dollar Silvertone. He drove a tractor on the Plantation for twenty-two cents an hour. Each night, he turned his shack into a honky-tonk. He said it was open, "from can 'til can't." Plantation workers in overalls tracked in gumbolike mud and stood along the bar. The crazies drank canned heat: Sterno strained with a handkerchief, a jolt that sent them reeling like a popped balloon. Muddy played his Silvertone for the crowd. He also ran a card game. Now and then, a shark took the entire pot. Some of the men carried a mojo hand: a red flannel bag fixed by a voodoo doctor, doused in oil and perfume, pierced with lucky needles. "You got a Mojo hand and you're gambling, you win," Muddy later said. "If you're after girls, you can work that mojo on any woman you want."

The sort of Delta honky-tonk where farmhands drank canned heat, sterno strained with a handkerchief. Muddy Waters said his was open, "From can 'til can't." (William R. Ferris Collection #20367, Box P-20367/4, CP-5-76-6, Southern Folklife Collection, Willson Library, University of North Carolina at Chaple Hill)

Lomax recorded Muddy in the fields behind his shack. Muddy was odd looking, regal. His forehead was high and furrowed in a way that denotes intelligence. His eyes were almond shaped, Eastern, the eyes of a Mongol king. His nose was broad and spread across his face like a spill. His mustache looked like it had been drawn with eyebrow pencil, two mustaches in fact, cleaved like Koreas, sloping into a new kind of punctuation mark that means *easy boy*. This scene, Muddy in the fields with Lomax, singing into a little microphone, should give you a sense of the tremendous sweep of his career. Here was Muddy as a stand-in for Robert

Johnson, archived as a remnant of a vanishing world, a figure out of Walker Evans; thirty years later he would turn up in Technicolor in *The Last Waltz,* the film directed by Martin Scorsese. Muddy was the athlete who crosses from one era into the next. He played "I Be's Troubled" and "Country Blues," the latter a song taken from Robert Johnson's version of "Walking Blues," a Delta staple. Everyone played "Walking Blues," the way every bar mitzvah band plays "Three Times a Lady." These numbers were haunting in the sell-your-soul style, with the aching repetition of the lyric "Minutes feel like hours, hours feel like days. Minutes feel like hours, hours feel like days."

A few months later, Lomax sent copies of the record to the Stovall Plantation. For Muddy, listening to the record came as a revelation. For the first time, he realized he could pull it off. He was just as good as any of them. "Never heard my voice on records, man, and to hear it was great," he later said. "That was one of the great things of my life." He played the disc again and again, his shack lit up like a lantern, music spilling from the windows— it must've been like the first time a kid discovers a mirror: the confusion, the recognition, the first burst of self-consciousness. He was ruined for the Delta. The cities down the line took on a concrete reality: he could go there, he could live there, he could play. He signed up with a traveling variety show called "Silas Green from New Orleans." He crisscrossed the country, playing at fairs and carnivals. He backed Blues acts on harmonica and sometimes sang. When the season ended, he went back to Stovall, kicked around, then left for good, lit out like old Nigger Jim, only the other direction along the river. When you read of this departure, it does indeed sound like Muddy was a slave in flight: he practically had to sneak away, ditching work, putting on his only suit, creeping across the fields to the train—that's how it was for a Negro tenant who had run up too much debt at the company store. And just like that, Mississippi was where it belonged: rolling backward in the window of a train. It's the sort of date they should make kids memorize: Muddy Waters arrived in Chicago at 9:30 a.m. on a Saturday in May 1943.

Muddy moved from house to house, spending days or weeks on the floors and couches of friends or relatives, distant cousins and long-lost aunts who fluffed up pillows or stitched quilts, asking after people back home, and of course covered whole tables in fried chicken and okra and cornbread and corn, so much like the Jewish mothers on the West Side, and Muddy sitting each night on the porch or fire escape with his guitar, staring over the rooftops and chimneys and exhaust fans at the haze that hangs over the city. He settled in a house on West 13th Street across from a vacant lot. He got a job in a container factory. He was one of those big farmhands from the South, heavy gloves and grease-smeared jeans and lunch breaks out of doors, long views across the lake. Each night he was at house parties with his guitar, playing for the crowds songs that sound like the old country—sharecropper music. He soon moved on to the dives, where he played with musicians with whom he would make his career: Sunnyland Slim, Jimmy Rogers, Little Walter. A generation on the edge, living to the very limit, neither wanting nor finding the comfortable middle ground, giving every bit away each night in the dives, back at work in the morning. Muddy landed his first full-time gig at the Flame Club on Indiana Avenue. Fifty-two dollars a week to moan and play bottleneck on a beat-up acoustic which could hardly be heard over the din.

Did Muddy Waters dream of bigger things? Yes, yes of course. There is a tendency, because Muddy played folk music—because, when he sings, he sounds like the voice of a lost people—to regard him as the sort of artifact that can only be discovered in the way the Grand Canyon was discovered but can never work for its own fame: if fame does come, and probably it should not come until the person is very old or very dead, it should come only by accident: Jerry Wexler turning up in Algiers. In other words, to be discovered is to be authentic; to search for fame is to be phony. So goes the logic of the aficionado. When it comes to the Blues, I have my own rule: if an artist believes what he is singing, he is authentic; if he does not believe what he is singing, even if he thinks it the prettiest idea in the world, he is not authentic. Charley Patton singing of Judgment Day believes that day will be penciled in early next week, and you hear it in his voice, and it has the spooky ring of authenticity. Taj Mahal singing the same song forty years later, technically a much better version, seems to regard Judgment Day as a story from literature, or a symbol, and so sounds not very authentic. Muddy Waters believed what he was singing and at the same time was ferociously ambitious. He was authentic and old schooly and also a product of the modern market. In other words, Leonard Chess might have been searching for Muddy Waters, but Muddy Waters was also searching for Leonard Chess.

Muddy began to make his name on the scene, each week attracting a few dozen more fans to the Flame Club, but the big moment came only when he started hanging around the Musicians Union Hall, where guitarists and pianists loitered like merchant seamen waiting for a ship. He was there with Sunnyland Slim when Sammy Goldberg, Leonard's scout at Aristocrat, came in. Goldberg wanted to hear Muddy, but Muddy did not have his guitar. Goldberg spotted Lonnie Johnson, who never went anywhere without his instrument. To Johnson, who played a sophisticated Blues, Muddy was a crude boy from the sticks. When Goldberg asked Johnson to borrow his guitar, Johnson said, "I don't lend my guitar. It's against my policy."

Goldberg said, "Come on, Lonnie, what the man gonna do? Eat your guitar?"

"Alright," said Johnson. "But just this once. It's a break in my policy."

Muddy Waters playing for Sammy Goldberg in the Musicians Union Hall—it's like Mick and Keith meeting on a train platform outside London, or Bob Dylan plugging in at the Newport Folk Festival, one of the dramatic set pieces of Rock & Roll. Because I have read so many descriptions of this scene, because it's always depicted in such a conventional way, because Rock & Roll has been for me and my friends the closest thing to a real faith, I like to imagine it in stained glass, a gospel story on the wall of a church off the Palisades Parkway in New Jersey: Muddy with a borrowed guitar, the crooked walls of the Musicians Union Hall, which, when the music plays, fall away like the walls of Jericho (not Long Island), revealing a wild El Greco sky where everything is happening at once, stars and moon and big blue sun dragging its sorry ass over the lake, the sound from the guitar indicated by a spray of orange shards—the music can be seen. And so strange in this city of the North, like an echo of an ancient slave rebellion that was never put down.

LEONARD CHESS HAD just turned forty. He had two children and was living on the South Shore of Chicago. Each new station in his life would be marked by a new house, a new office. It's one of the places where the Jewish character and the American character bleed into one, this rootlessness, this urge to roam: *how can you tell you are moving if the scenery doesn't change?* Leonard truly became Leonard only at forty. As a young man, he seems miscast, itchy in the too-tight costume of youth, a man who craves the authority of middle-age—papa, with his brood and mind made up and voice so much like the rumble of a bass guitar. Leonard fully realized: a man who knows when to shout and when to whisper; who, though balding, never attempts a comb-over; who, though graying, never attempts a dye, and wears bland suits and blah shirts and lets his eyes carry the weight of expression. A man who sits on his desk, folds his arms, lets his head roll back and says, "We take care of this problem now, or it takes care of us later."

On his way to work, you could not pick him out from the crowd of nine-to-fivers. A face in a sea of faces, how could you know he hid among them like Oppenheimer, building a lab to split the atom. Coffee, donut, *Sun-Times,* galoshes. Leonard was a progressive in a (not really) progressive town; a Democrat in a city of machine-built Democrats. When he made millions, he would

Leonard Chess, the macher, the schnorrer, the tough Polish Jew, in the 1950s. Where others saw a horde, he saw a market. (Michael Ochs Archives.com)

give it away by the tens of thousands to charity—that classic chow mein of Jewish philanthropy, half to Israel, half to everyone else, mostly blacks, NAACP, CORE. He might seem old-fashioned, a relic of the pre-Kennedy, hat-wearing era, but he was in fact a true modern, a pioneer in a business as new as the Internet is today. In this, he followed a long tradition of Jews who sought their fortunes in the brand-new thing, often in that place where show biz intersects with technology. It was the age of the Jewish photographer, the Jewish filmmaker. Such men placed their faith in progress because what did they have to be nostalgic for, because show me an invention and I will show you a way to get rich, because a new technology is inevitably followed by a new industry that has not had time to build the barriers to keep out men like Leonard Chess.

For Leonard, this was an era of long days, the sort well known to our fathers and grandfathers but not to us. He would spend seven, eight hours in the office, or in the studio, or hustling distributors, then head to the Macomba, which he had mostly left for Phil to run. The life of the club owner was something Leonard left behind, the noise and violence drifting into lore. In 1948, Charles Aron, co-owner of Aristocrat, divorced his wife, Evelyn. Leonard, with ten grand borrowed from his father, bought out Charles Aron's share. Leonard now had a stake in the gold mine. He was an owner. A capitalist.

So what kind of a record man was Leonard?

Up to this point, he had flown on the prevailing winds, producing flat jazzed-up Blues that sounded like everything else; records that came and went like wind across the sand. Fire-spotting trends, anticipating the next break in a wave, talent scouting his way up the charts (shit, shit, shit, *hit,* shit)—these were not Leonard's skills. He was no genius. He did not dazzle into the big score. He instead had to work for it, fake it, steal it, copy it, shuffle and fight. He was smart and tough in the way of the hard worker, the long-distance runner, the gambler who wins on stamina. In business, and probably in art too, such men have the advantage over the genius, who depends on the great big nothing, a fluky, unpredictable freak. One day it's there and one day it's gone back to whatever nowhere it came from, and you are like the card sharp who bets on instinct when his luck runs out, with no way to fake your way back into the game. But for the hard worker, it is a fake from the beginning, and so he's developed a million tricks and bluffs to get through. Leonard could not spot a song, something he was criticized and mocked for, but he had a skill far more important: he could spot the man who could spot the song, woo him and hire him, and then, when the gift goes away, dump him like an aging wife. It was not music Leonard had a talent for—it was people. A bloodsucking skill because, if done right, it means, in a business sense, never growing old. Willie Dixon would serve as the key man in the glory years, but in the beginning it was Sammy Goldberg. And it was Goldberg who, one day when a musician did not turn up for a session, remembered the kid he had met in the union hall: Muddy Waters.

"I never during all those Chess years looked upon my father or my uncle or myself as artists," Marshall Chess told me. "We were businessmen trying to make it. My father wanted to make what black people wanted to buy. We were not out to make great music. We were out to make hits, to make money. And that's what the artists wanted."

When the call came, Muddy was out on the truck—he had a job delivering venetian blinds. The relative who took the message got in his car and raced around the city looking for Muddy, another moment so crucially cinematic you imagine it in storyboard: jagged lines, narrow streets, the big truck tearing around a corner. When Muddy got the message, he ran to a phone and called his boss. He said his cousin had been found dead in an alley and he had to rush home. This lie is the original sin on which Muddy built his career—OK, not a deal with the Devil, but still pretty graphic and ghetto-y in a way meant to titillate the white boss. So here comes Muddy, and this guy walks like John Wayne, a soldier back from the war, a farmer in the rain, drenched but not about to hurry. His first recordings were a classic case of trying too hard, aping the Bluebird beat. In the second or third session, after he had burned up considerable tape and money, and the patience of Leonard was wearing thin—and as a Negro from the South Muddy could always sense the loss of patience in a white man—he figured, *Fuck it, if I fail at least I will fail as myself,* and launched into some old Delta Blues. This is the moment the needle, after popping and hissing, falls into the groove and the music blasts away—a song that will play for the next thirty years. Two sides came out of the session: "I Can't Be Satisfied" and "Feel Like Going Home," basically the same songs Muddy had recorded for Alan Lomax.

Leonard did not get this music. Every time Muddy sang a verse, Leonard would ask, "What is he saying? What the fuck is he saying?" He would ask this in the same way that, on trips in the Toyota Celica, when I played my tapes, usually by the Clash or R.E.M., but also the Alarm and Mojo Nixon and Tom Petty, my father would slap the dashboard and say, "Where in the name of Sweet Pete is the melody?" This was just before my father replaced my tape ("Road Mix Two") with Sinatra's "Old Blue Eyes Is Back," saying, "Now that's music!" Or: "When Frank says, 'The summer went so quickly,' he is not talking about the summer, he is talking about life. It's life that goes so quickly." And then Leonard said, "Who's going to buy that?" This question, unlike, "What the fuck is he saying," or, "Where in the name of Sweet Pete is the melody," would soon be answered to Leonard's satisfaction.

When the record was cut, Leonard kept it on the shelf. Muddy came in week after week to ask when it would hit stores. Leonard said, "Patience" or "Give it time" or "Wait your turn." Over the years, this became the habit at Chess. If Leonard was your boyfriend, you would call him commitment-phobic: he recorded and recorded but seemed never to release. He blanched when it came time to plunge, invest the money, press, and distribute. A record would spend years in larval form as an acetate, the big waxy master from which copies were made. For every four songs recorded, maybe one was put into production. To suspicious artists like Bo Diddley or Jimmy Rogers, it seemed a form of control, with the songs held as hostages. Leonard said he was in fact protecting his investment, guarding the reputation of his artists by only releasing quality—an assertion scoffed at until Leonard died and many of those shelf-bound originals were released. In 1997, Jimmy Rogers told *Living Blues* magazine, "I hear some stuff they released on Muddy Waters, it's terrible, man. I made lots of stuff. I hope they don't ever release it." At times, it seemed Leonard was awaiting a portent or an omen. He tended to rely on oracles. Sonny Woods, who worked in the stock room, would listen to each new cut, saying, "This ain't shit" or "Put that motherfucker out." When Sonny Woods first heard "High-Heeled Sneakers," he said, "Let's get it on the street." And also those random individuals, like the blowzy neighborhood lady who was standing out of the weather under the front awning when Leonard put on the acetate of Little Walter's "Juke." The music drifted through the rain and the woman started to clap her hands and dance. The record was rushed into production.

But these songs by Muddy—no one had ever made commercial records like this. It was music from the underclass, the language of rent parties and cotton fields. *Who the fuck is going to buy that?* In the end, it was not Leonard who had the guts to press and release—it was Evelyn Aron. She was in the business less for the money than for the connection to the real, and these songs were real. It was Evelyn who pushed Leonard to release that first record by Muddy. "Evelyn was the one who really liked my stuff," Waters said. "Leonard didn't know nothing about the blues, but Evelyn, she really got it."

A few thousand copies of "I Can't Be Satisfied" were released in the summer of 1948. "This was old deep Delta blues, no doubt, but it was also something new," Robert Palmer writes in *Deep Blues*. "It stood out amid the glut of sax-led jump combos and balladeers because of its simplicity, passion, and hypnotic one-chord droning." Of course, with songs, as with people, context is everything. The passage of time can diminish or enhance a song, or change it into something else. A tune that was crap when new, like "Wang Chung," returns years later as a time capsule, which, if it catches you unaware, will knock you out. For a few weeks you revel in it, feeding off its flavor of the past, until you bleed it out like gum and so bring it back into today, where once again it's crap. Songs that, on first release, were good but probably not mysterious, like early George Jones or Johnny Cash, are remade by time into hints of a vanished America, spooky in the way of old photographs. "In Dreams" by Roy Orbison was surely excellent when new but could not have carried that charge that sends the malaise needles deep into the red. Other songs are diminished by time, and this is often the case with the Blues, which have been so ripped off and imitated they've become almost impossible to hear. Time has made them into background noise, like a ragtime tune used in a documentary about the Jazz Age, so you must really work to hear them as they sounded in those first years, the novelty and charge and sex and dirt of them. How strange to hear "Feel Like Going Home" in 1948 after years of the bland pop on the Hit Parade. "The first guitarist I was ever aware of was Muddy Waters," Jimi Hendrix is quoted as saying in *Crosstown Traffic: Jimi Hendrix & Post-War Pop,* by Charles Shaar Murray. "I heard one of his early records when I was a little boy, and it scared me to death."

It was this music that would set up the collision between poor blacks and middle-class whites that would result in Rock & Roll. For the first generation of rock stars, hearing these Blues was a revelation. "It changed everything," Eric Clapton told *Rolling Stone.* "Muddy was the first person that got to me and his is still the most important music in my life." For those who loved the music but could not play, these records drew forth that cataract of articles and books that suggests a cultural shift—wherever you see a cloud of paper, something big has happened. The music ushered in a super dorky school of music writing, educated white guys picking apart the thoughts and lyrics of poor black guys. Here is John Collis, in his book *Chess Records,* summing up the plot of

the Muddy Water's song "Louisiana Blues": "The singer is yearn-
ing for Louisiana as an escape route from his troubles and to equip
himself with a 'mojo hand' to ensure greater sexual success."

Leonard placed Muddy's record in stores across the South
Side, in groceries and beauty salons and newsstands, where he
hoped people would recognize Muddy's name from the dives.
This is the part of the story where I am supposed to say this
record, which the boss did not want to release, a record without
precedent, made by a mostly illiterate black man (Muddy *could*
sign his name) who, until a few years before, lived in a shack on
the edge of a cotton field, became a surprise, runaway hit—and
so it did! On the morning of its release, when Muddy walked to
Maxwell Street to buy a copy, he was told, because the record
was selling so fast, customers were allowed only two copies.
Muddy bought two and sent his wife back for two more. There
was no radio, no advertising, no nothing. It was word of mouth.
Leonard had stumbled upon a vast reserve: over a hundred thousand blacks from Mississippi who craved their own music. For
everyone else, it was a change in the weather, an appearance of
the real, Brando mumbling in a movie. It was like that commercial: she told two friends, and she told two friends, and so on,
and so on. The record sold out by the end of the first day. Leonard
pressed thousands more. He did not analyze this success or take
it apart—he simply did what good merchants do: played out the
string, not caring why it worked, just glad it did. He stayed with
it until it redefined him: switched the label from sophisticated
Blues to a down-home sound. Leonard was now the impresario
of Delta Blues, music sold to the poorest people in the city. He

began signing the artists, most of them from Mississippi, who would turn his company into a powerhouse: Robert Nighthawk, Robert Little John, Little Milton, Clarence Gatemouth Brown, John Lee Hooker. Muddy's record went on to sell over sixty thousand copies, many more than any other record ever released by Aristocrat. It reached top twenty in Billboard.

For Muddy, it was a strange sensation. Fame. As if he had cast off an image that had gone on to live a life of its own. *What did it have to do with him?* Late one night, he was driving alone through the city in his new convertible, the streets shut down and the windows dark and the dark towers like a distant line of hills, and that warm wind that blows all summer, and he heard a sound so forlorn and familiar he pulled over and sat for a long moment listening before he realized it was his own voice, his own song, floating down from the dark apartments above. "And it really scared me," he said. "I thought I had died."

MUDDY WATERS PIONEERED the new sound in the clubs on the South Side. The Flame Club, the Checkerboard. In addition to his fee, he was given an open line on Hennessey. During wild numbers, he would jam a soda bottle in his pants and shake it and pull it and pop it and spray it across the girls who crowded close to the stage. The sound of the dives—a sound that evolved from the Delta Blues, that picked up the steely jump of the city as it moved north, the rattle of street corners and stoops, the slaughter yards, the loading docks, the assembly lines. Muddy traded his Coke bottle slide for a piece of steel tubing a friend had swiped from a factory—a perfect symbol of his switch from the plantation to the big town, where musicians plugged in because it was the only way to be heard in the clubs. As their life grew noisier, so did their songs, until the noise itself became the point, the industrial wail of the city refashioned as music.

Of course, this new sound would depend entirely on the electric guitar, and the electric guitar did not make its appearance until the 1940s, a result of the same process that brought the phonograph and the telephone. The first electric guitars were Spanish acoustics fitted with hookups to amplify sound. The modern solid body appeared only in 1950: the Fender Esquire. For those who played these instruments, the big obstacle was feedback, that screech you hear at school assemblies and political rallies, wherever an instrument or voice is fed through an amplifier. Many innovations were driven by a desire to defeat feedback. But for Muddy, the breakthrough came when he decided, *Why fight it, why not just play it?* "The effect of electricity is rather awe-inspiring," novelist and musicologist Samuel Charters wrote in *The Country Blues.* "The men sweating over their instruments, the sound ringing over the din of the crowd." The realization that you could actually play the noise marks the birth of a new music. You go from there to the hard licks of Chuck Berry, to the single-string guitar solos of Neil Young, in which he actually seems to surf on electricity, to the wild, ear-splitting fuzz of Nirvana.

The history of music, like the history of history, is a struggle between theories: great men versus great events. Yes, there were pioneers in the business, Muddy Waters and Elvis Presley, and

Leonard Chess and Ahmet Ertegun, but there is also a more mechanistic way of looking at this. In 1950, you had the first modern electric guitar. In 1955, you had Rock & Roll. *If not Napoleon, some other scrappy Frenchman would have gone after the Russians.* For the first time, it was possible for a guitar to be a lead instrument, the center of the new music the way the trumpet and the saxophone were at the center of Jazz. In the past, a band was usually built around a booming piano, which is loud enough to be heard in the concert halls and saloons; with the infusion of electricity, which was in some way equivalent to the close-up in motion pictures—it brought even the smallest gestures to the fore—three or four players (drummer, bassist, guitarist) could dominate a crowded bar. The whine of the electric guitar—a sound that would run like a line through modern music, from the early experiments of Chet Atkins and Les Paul, to the *wham bam* of Chuck Berry and Eddie Cochran, to Scotty Moore haunting the empty space behind Elvis. For me, the music hits its groove with the surf tunes of the early sixties, a brief moment before the Beatles blew everything away—songs by Dick Dale, and the Ventures, and Link Ray, guitars crashing like waves, the cool run after the hard work is over. "Apache," "Forty Miles of Bad Road," "Slaughter on Tenth Avenue"—songs that make you think of a dozen places: the Glencoe beach five minutes before sundown, a road in Wisconsin that twists through the trees, the roller coaster at the end of the pier in Santa Cruz.

Muddy Waters formed the first truly electric band on the South Side of Chicago. He sang and played guitar in this band, but there was also Jimmy Rogers, born in 1924 in Ruleville, Mississippi, moved to Atlanta, St. Louis, Memphis, where he played for "all the whiskey I could drink." Rogers created the template for the George Harrison type, the studious, superaccomplished musician who gets overlooked. He played second guitar in Muddy's band, the rhythm lost behind the slashing slide. Yet it was this rhythm that stands as a great legacy of the electric Blues, the driving sound swiped by every modern group. Rogers gave the music its tremendous swagger. He was fresh-faced and smooth and wore dark suits and skinny ties. His sound set in motion a chain of events that follows as logically, one to another, as the weightier points in history: no Napoleon no Bismarck, no Bismarck no Germany, no Germany no Hitler, no Hitler no Holocaust, no Holocaust no Israel. *No Napoleon no Israel.* No Jimmy Rogers no Muddy Waters band, no Muddy Waters band no Beatles, no Beatles no Woodstock, no Woodstock no Bill Clinton. *No Jimmy Rogers no Bill Clinton.*

"I listened to Muddy and said, 'I know what he needs,'" Rogers told *Living Blues.* "Like if you don't have enough salt in your food, it don't taste right. You need more. So I added sound— what he was singing, that's the way I would play." Rogers cut his own sides ("Ludella," "That's Alright"), but it's his work with Muddy that set the stage for Keith Richards and Pete Townshend, for all those white boys who would copy a sound that was, in fact, an echo of the Illinois Central leaving towns with names like Ruleville.

The other great player was Little Walter Jacobs, who used to jam with Rogers on Jew Street. By running his harmonica through an amplifier, Walter changed the sound of the Blues and helped invent Rock & Roll. Of all the pioneers, he is my favorite. Because his harmonica was a defining sound, because he lived to play, because Miles Davis told Marshall Chess Little Walter was "one of the greatest musical geniuses of his time." And also because he was a sharp dresser, was boastful and easily offended and jumpy as hell; because, when he cupped a harmonica and closed his eyes and played one of his dazzling riffs, which sound to me more like Chicago than even the elevated train, he looked just great; because before him the harmonica was hardly considered an instrument, but after him whole songs were built around it; because his face was clean and handsome at a distance but up close seasoned with knife scars won by his temper in the dives; because he actually lived the sort of epic life people like Bob Dylan fake in interviews and conjure up in songs like "Tangled Up In Blue."

Little Walter was born in Marksville, Louisiana, in 1930. He grew up like a stray dog. When he was twelve, he ran away to New Orleans, one of those street urchins you see around Jackson Square, working the grift. When he was fourteen, he wandered off across the country, surviving scrapes and adventures. He was too young to play in the joints, and the roads were dark in the country at night, the moon on the fields. He turned up in Helena, Arkansas, where he lived on the street and in taverns where the Blues were booming. Sometimes he slept on a pool table. He hung around the stars of the scene, Robert Nighthawk and Robert Junior Lockwood, the (sort of) stepson of Robert Johnson. He would jump on stage between sets and play. He learned a lot from Rice Miller, Sonny Boy Williamson II, who played harmonica each afternoon on the radio for *King Biscuit Time*. Sonny Boy

*Postcards featuring young Sonny Boy Williamson, playing his harp
and selling someone else's biscuits.* (Gladin Collection, Southern Media Archive,
University of Mississippi Special Collections)

proved the instrument could be expressive and full throated, not something you had to grow out of. Walter learned more from the saxophone player Louis Jordan, who he heard on the radio. Walter mimicked Jazz solos on the harp, which seemed to many as pointless as passing a basketball between your legs. By cross-pollination, he stumbled onto something new. When Jimmy Rogers met Little Walter in 1947 on Maxwell Street, he was plugged into an amp, the first musician to electrify a harmonica, to run it through a speaker, which created a new instrument, as uncertain as the human voice, a howl that lit up the depths. Walter was sixteen when Rogers introduced him to Muddy. "When I run up on Little Walter, he just fitted me," Muddy later said. "He had this thing on harp nobody ever had. They're still trying for it today, but they can't never come up close to it."

This was the first Rock & Roll band, though it was not yet called that. It was the loudest music anyone ever heard. It had the drive of an engine, the hum of a diesel on an inky black night— music that makes you feel like staying out late, driving too fast, drinking more than is advisable, starting a fight. The Devil's music, the great enabler behind all the half-witted schemes you cook up after your fifth Hennessey. In *The Country Blues,* Samuel Charters described the audience at one of the live shows: "A tough, sleek, crowd that drinks hard, wants its music hard and fills the small dark club with an intense mood of restlessness." He then describes the band: "Drunk and tired, clothes limp with sweat, they sit with their faces quiet, fingers moving over the guitar strings with a sad, mournful blues sound. The music is best when it gets toward morning." It's the swagger, the con, the determined face you turn into the wind. Behind it is the realization that makes Rock & Roll possible: attitude is everything. It's Little Walter on "Boom, Boom Out Goes the Lights":

No kidding, I'm ready to fight
I just saw my baby last night
If I get her in my sights
Boom Boom out go the lights

Little Walter got his break in 1952, when, with time left over in a recording session, Muddy decided the band should cut one more tune, a nameless riff they played at the end of each set in their live show. It was a theme song. Everyone played on it, but since it featured a jumpy harmonica solo, and since Walter had no songs to his credit, Muddy decided to give it to the kid. Leonard called it "Juke." The band went on tour soon after it was released. It was a hit by the time they reached the South. One day, when a fan did not treat Walter with what Walter deemed proper respect for an artist with a hit, he got bent out of shape and bothered and in essence said to Waters and Rogers, *So long suckers.* Little Walter went back to Chicago and formed his own band. He was soon in the studio with Leonard, beginning a ten-year run that produced many classics: "Blues with a Feeling," "Roller Coaster," "Keys to the Highway." His biggest hit was "My Babe," which Willie Dixon wrote for Little Walter because "Little Walter was always bragging about his girl, and what he's got is better than what you got."

It was this feistiness that broke up the Muddy Waters band,

and that, everyone knew, would someday be the end of Little Walter. As the gamblers say, *You might be the King of Hearts, but somewhere in that deck is the Ace of Spades.* On Valentine's Day 1968, when Walter was thirty-eight, he was playing dice on the street and an argument broke out. Walter grabbed the money and the other man hit him in the head with a pipe. Walter went home, lay down, and never woke up. And so, all these years later, on the streets of Chicago, Walter Jacobs was killed by Old Stagger Lee.

MUDDY WANTED TO BRING his band into the studio, but Leonard fought it. Leonard fought everything. It was his money, and unlike a major label he could not afford a single misstep. That's why he took so long to press a new release, why he counted each penny and squeezed each dime. He had the panicky hoarding instinct of one who's come through the Depression. He was not deterred by the stereotype of the miserly Jew—if there's a little change left on the plate, better him than you. Besides, Aristocrat was still doing quite well with Muddy's solo records. And it's the first rule of good business: don't fuck with a cocktail that's getting you drunk. What's more, with Muddy alone on acoustic, Leonard had just one musician to coddle, encourage, discourage, pay. With a band—Muddy was playing with Jimmy Rogers, Little Walter, and Baby Face Leroy Foster on drums—Leonard would quadruple his cost.

It was not until 1950 that Leonard agreed to bring the Muddy Waters band into the studio, minus drums (a last nagging attachment to the uncluttered sound of country Blues). Typically, the family would later credit Leonard with introducing the very sound he at first kept out. "My father wanted drum, drum, and more drum," Marshall told me. "I think he was responsible for doing that to the Blues, bringing in that heavy beat"—a quote that makes one fact plain: sons love their fathers. It also suggests what was probably Leonard's best quality: the ease with which he got clear of his own bad decisions and appropriated whatever was working. He does not want to record Delta Blues; then, when it sells, it's the only thing he wants to record. Ditto electric Blues; ditto drums.

Which raises the question: just what did Leonard Chess bring to the music? If he resisted each innovation, if he wanted to do only what had already been done, then what did his presence mean to the Blues? What can any businessman bring to a field that is essentially artistic? A question that has forever pitched Medicis against Michaelangelos, Selznicks against Hitchcocks. Yes, Leonard brought money and equipment and salesmanship, but it was more than just a case of the fat kid happens to own the basketball. It was no accident that within a few years of telling Muddy to ditch his drummer, Leonard had produced the greatest roster of drum-heavy Blues in history. He might be slow to get something, but once he got it, he got behind it, and stayed behind it, until it worked. He was the father in the bleachers at the game he at first did not want his son to play. "He was a firm knothead," Malcolm Chisholm, who worked at the label, was quoted as saying in *I Am the Blues*, the autobiography of Willie Dixon. "But, to his credit, when he thought something was right, he'd go for it."

Muddy Waters and Otis Spann in the 1950s. At Chess, Leonard created a safe haven for his artists. (© Terry Cryer/Corbis)

"Here was a guy with blind faith," Muddy is quoted as saying in *Spinning Blues into Gold,* by Nadine Cohodas. "He didn't believe in my blues when we started but he did believe in me. I got a huge kick out of proving myself to him. I got a kick out of the fact that more than business associates, we became intimate friends. I tell everyone that the one person responsible for my success is Leonard."

Mostly, Leonard created a safe haven where musicians could do their best work. In the unpredictable wilds of the record industry, he fostered a sense of stability. He was the adult, the man in charge, which amounted to a kind of charisma: not the charisma of the rock star, but the charisma of the father, the man the dog runs to, the man you seek out when the papers are served. "Chess was phenomenal," Alan Duncan, who worked at the label, was quoted as saying in *I Am the Blues*. "He was a brain but what made it was the cat had this magnetic personality. He'd be grinning and telling you how great you were and laughing all the way to the bank."

"The blues and gospel people would rather sign with Chess than with the other companies," Ron Malo said in *I Am the Blues*. "If they were going to get screwed, they would rather get screwed by Leonard, because Leonard at least was honest about it."

"Leonard did so much for blues," said Jimmy Rogers. "At that time, he was the only one getting this music out. And I guess you could say blues did so much for him, too."

The career of Leonard can in fact be divided into stages: the early years, when he was hunting acts, guessing, risking, gambling. And the golden years, when his label gained a sort of critical mass, a gravity that sucked in all the wandering comets and asteroids and space junk: no longer would Leonard have to crisscross the country looking for artists—the talent would come looking for him. "Anybody Chess fool around with seems like he going to get the best out of," Johnny Shines told John Collis in *Chess Records*. "He had patience to work with a guy, find out what he react to. I might've hooked up with twenty-five other labels, but I wanted to go with Chess."

The Muddy Waters band was in the studio for hours, cutting tracks that would form the foundation of Rock & Roll—like a sequence shot by one of the great American directors, John Ford or Sam Peckinpah, a battlefield scene of drifting smoke and voices. The camera comes in low, picking up every stain and butt in the carpet, and someone has been smoking a joint, and the men look huge, are huge, Muddy draining a bottle of whiskey, hitting his guitar, *bam!* The feedback clearing his head, Little Walter dropping to his knees, and we see each pore and bead of sweat and knife scar as he blasts his harp into the control booth, where Leonard sucks cigarettes to the knuckle, shouting, *Play, motherfucker, play!*

The men emerge in the early morning. Leonard crosses the street, gets in his car, roars off. The band stumbles away like hobos, wrecked but one more drink to toast the songs in the can—"She Moves Me," "Long Distance Call," "Honey Bee"— Muddy making his guitar sound like an angry swarm of yellow jackets. When these records hit, they hit like M80s. Loud, jarring, wild. The black radio stations are alive with it: *And now, Muddy Waters and his band!* A few weeks after its release, "Louisiana Blues" reached the top ten in *Billboard*. Critics heralded it as a new music. "There was a kind of frenzy and extra vulgarity to rhythm & blues that had not been present in the older blues forms," LeRoi Jones writes in *Blues People*. "Suddenly it was as if a great deal of the Euro-American humanist façade in African American music had been washed away." People loved to fuck to this music, drink to it, get high to it, and listen to it as the sun went down over the prairie.

4

2120 South Michigan

In 1950, Evelyn Aron, who never really liked her partner, who saw him as a graspy, grubbing, scheming, plotting vulgarian and she was right, and that is what made him great, sold out. Leonard was now the sole owner of the label, which, until the end of his career, he would run by fiat. When Phil came over full-time, he did everything Leonard did—signed bands, produced records, pitched distributors—in fact, it would never have worked without Phil and the special dynamic of the brothers' working in combination—but Leonard was the big boss, having the same advantages over the majors, with their floors and floors of bureaucracy, that a monarchy has over a democracy. "Normally you have a command structure with a president on top and different departments," Ron Malo said in *I Am the Blues*. "Chess was a bicycle wheel. Leonard at the hub and everything circling around him. He would fix the toilets himself rather than pay a plumber $6.95 to replace a valve."

At the suggestion of a record presser named Buster Williams,

Leonard changed the name of the company. Aristocrat struck the wrong note for a label recording rough electric Blues. Leonard must have also felt a need to mark his emergence as an independent operator. Chess was the family name, and it also had a nice top-drawer ring. Leonard would eventually form subsidiary labels—like the imprints book publishers use to denote different genres: there was Chess, which recorded Blues; Checker, which recorded Pop and Rock and Blues; and Argo, which recorded Jazz and comedy so blue it calls up a spit-take.

In the coming years, Leonard would move the company from office to office, studio to studio, forever working toward self-sufficiency. He was trying to make his independent into a major, a goal he nearly reached at 320 East 21st Street, the label's last home. It housed the business office, art department, recording studio, and pressing plant. In one building, Chess could sign and record, press and package and ship its records. But this turned out to be a lesson in unintended consequences. With the presses running, a hum went through the building and into the studio. You can hear it on the songs cut in those years, the building rumbling like an old school.

In the early years, Chess recorded in a series of makeshift studios. Technicians sought to dampen the defects of these rooms (padding walls, covering ducts), but it soon became clear that the defects were creating the sound the critics found so fresh. You can identify the era of a side by the studio where it was cut, the way you can identify a scotch by the keg in which it was aged. In the sessions recorded at 4750 South Cottage Grove, there is an echo that gives the sides a Rockabilly jump. This came to be known as the Chess sound, which the majors spent thousands trying to replicate. It was, in fact, the accidental result of a steel pipe that ran through the studio. "The [musicians] would put a speaker at one end of the pipe and a microphone at the other," said Marshall. "They would feed the sound out from the speaker, and it would travel along the pipe, and get picked up by the microphone with the echo from the pipe."

But the studio at 2120 South Michigan Avenue is what people mean when they talk about Chess Records. It's where many of the great songs were recorded; where Leonard, in his booth, shouted into a mic, "Play it likes it moves you, motherfucker"; where artists hung out for hours, trading guitar licks and dirty jokes; where Leonard hid from anyone he owed cash; where Leonard snuck Etta James out the back door a step ahead of the cops—she was wanted on drug charges. It's where rock bands from England came on pilgrimage. The Rolling Stones cut several sides in the studio, including "2120 South Michigan Ave," a happy-peppy version of a Little Walter riff. A few years ago, the building, which had fallen into ruin, was salvaged and turned into a museum by Willie Dixon. It's called Blues Heaven. There are guitars on the walls, gold records, T-shirts, books for sale, and the wooden stairs in back have been warped by thousands of trips up and down with heavy equipment. When I was there, the guide seemed impressed mostly by the size of the Chess artists. He said things like, "Muddy, now that was a big man." Or "Howlin' Wolf could hold you in the palm of his hand." On display in one room was a pair Willie Dixon's jeans nailed to a wall like a painting, and they were huge.

For Leonard, the old world disappeared in 1950, when the Macomba burned down. A convenient disaster. The brothers were looking for a way out—a nightclub was a dicey way to make a living—when, on a clear afternoon, *whoosh!* the sky clouded over and it rained insurance money. A fitting end for the lounge: no decline, no boarded windows, no crack house: booming, then gone, cauterized like a wound, left to fester only in memory. It marked the end of Leonard's early life and the beginning of his days as a mogul. If this were a movie, you would see the transition as a fancy dissolve, close on the fire, the crackling sound of flames, then fade to the whitewall tire of a speeding Cadillac—the crackle of flames is now the sound of car wheels on a gravel road.

LEONARD CHESS BUILT his empire on the road. He would set off every few months in his Cadillac. In each town, he would stop at the radio station and record distributor, the trunk filled with his latest release. He worked mostly on the wrong side of the tracks, in the bungalows and painted houses of the Negro quarter. Before Rock & Roll, Leonard made party records for Negroes. The numbers were small. A record that sold forty thousand copies was reason to celebrate. Such a record, which cost no more than ten grand to produce, might bring fifty grand in profit. "Fuck hits," Leonard is quoted as saying in Willie Dixon's *I Am the Blues*. "Give me thirty thousand on everything I put out." Once every two or three years, a record would sell eighty or ninety thousand copies—enough to carry all the losers, but, in the grand scheme, still no El Dorado. This is one reason men

like Leonard were able to find a place in an industry dominated
by behemoths. In the early years, the numbers were too small
to attract hostile attention from the majors. It was the sort of
skim that, in Vegas, the house hardly notices. "For an independent everything is cheaper," Julie Rifkin, an old-time record man,
told me. "It's like rap guys today. You go into a studio for a few
grand and come out with something you can sell. Twenty thousand copies means nothing to a major, but if you sell that in a regular kind of way, you get rich. And twenty thousand copies, that's
where the trends are—that's why the majors never break anything
new. At the start, the reward is too small. But they follow, and
when they follow, watch out, because they follow with money."

Leonard wore cotton pants and Miami Beach shirts, another
one of those middle-aged men who, when you pass them on the
highway in the South, seem like a piece of the North blown off
course. Such men, no one knows why, usually have two or three
hats on the deck below the rear window in their car. Leonard
was different on such trips: watchful, polite, less swearing, less
swaggering. In Chicago, he was surrounded by artists and acted
in a way he thought appropriate for artists. In creative fields,
executives tend to regard talent as freaks or as children, posses-
sors of an innate gift but helpless: the monkey fed by the organ
grinder. To a hard-nosed guy like Leonard, Sonny Boy was not a
black man in a white man's world; he was something far more
rarefied and malleable: a freakish conduit to the music, a baby
grown into a man and still the umbilical chord is uncut. "I have
a theory," Joe Smith told me. "Assume the human brain is made
of chips like a computer. And those chips govern behavior. Well,

these [musicians] can take a sheet of paper and put notes on it and go into a studio and translate it into music and perform that music in front of millions. We can't do that. They got chips we don't. But to make room for those chips, other chips fall out. Sanity, reason, logic, gratitude. Anything like that is gone. So if you understand they are not like you and I, then you're ok. They landed in a field in Iowa many years ago and some day will be called back home."

Asked if he treated artists like they were his children, Phil Chess, quoted in *Spinning Blues into Gold*, said, "Well, they wanted to be."

The executives feel superior to artists, but also envious—of the freedom, the talent, the lifestyle, the girls, girls, girls, the sprees, the benders, the crowds. Mario Medious, who, in the seventies, was sent on the road by Warner Brothers to keep Led Zeppelin out of trouble, told guitarist Jimmy Page that he slept with the skankiest groupies because, "You go in front of thousands of people and get off on stage. I gotta get mine the old-fashioned way." The artists were aware of this and so came to tease and test the executives, who wanted to make money but also had the old lunch-room need to be cool. By the 1970s, being a music executive meant partying just as hard as the stars, getting just as loaded, staying just as blasted. Members of the Grateful Dead syringed LSD into a Coke can and gave it to the promoter Bill Graham, who spent the rest of the night dancing on stage with a tambourine. It was a reverse version of *Invasion of the Body Snatchers*: one after another, these buttoned-down businessman turned up in tie-dye.

Bob Krasnow, who built Elektra Records into a powerhouse, told me how he landed Metallica: "I was at Jerry's Bar & Grill with my friend Shep Gordon and Les Garland, who was then program director for *MTV*," said Krasnow. "We were having dinner and, OK, yes, fine, drinking tequila, and Metallica was opening at Roseland. My friend had gotten this brand new pill called Halcion and he said, 'This is the greatest pill because it doesn't give you a hangover.' And he gave me this pill and I took this pill. By the time I see Metallica, I can barely walk, or keep my eyes open, or anything. I was being propped up, babbling God knows what, out of it. Tequila and Halcion, what a combination! Shep gets me out of there in one piece. Les comes out and throws up all over my chauffeur. The next day I get to the office and say, 'I think I saw Metallica last night.' So I call the guys and they say, 'Oh yeah, we remember you. You were that guy falling all over the place. We love that, man.' So I signed them."

The record man is different than other businessmen. He inhabits a place between commerce and art. A bohemian with a chauffeur. A man who tells his secretary, "Willie is great, but I pretty much wrote the whole fucking thing." He is Ahmet Ertegun playing a tape that proves he composed one of the great Ray Charles songs. He is Marshall Chess saying, "My father wanted drum, drum, and more drum." The creative executive—a baggy term used by record men to define their position. Not to say these men do not contribute, because they do; not to say they are not unique, because they are; but mostly because, unlike most other businessmen, they deal not with a service or product, but with the most difficult, drugged up self-important item in the world—

rock stars. Bands rise and fall, trends come and go, but the record man goes on forever.

Leonard drove around twenty thousand miles a year. In the fifties, he began taking Marshall on these trips. Heading south from Chicago is like getting sucked down a drain, past acres of factories and car dealerships into the creepy land of acid ponds. "There was a story in *Billboard* when I was ten or eleven," Marshall told me. "It said, 'Leonard is taking his son on the road to teach him the business.' But really, that was just how he spent time with me; he took me to work." After hours behind the wheel, the white line swinging before his eyes like a pocket watch, the fields bleeding into a wash of color, faces and shapes appearing up the road, old friends and dead relatives, the ship that brought you to America, the train that took you to Chicago, Big Gene taking that knife in the Macomba, Leonard would slap himself hard on the back of the neck, pull over, fields gathered around like empty bleachers—in a place like this, you feel the eyes on you—get into the backseat and say to Marshall, "Drive." Marshall was too young to drive and scared. He steered onto the empty road, slow at first, then, his father snoring in back, let her unwind, blasting through that dead country, giggling like mad.

They would stop at sheet-music stores to see what records were selling. They would go into taverns, where Marshall sat on a stool with a Coke as Leonard tried to convince the owner to carry his record in the jukebox. They would go to joints in search of talent. "We taped guys in cotton fields," Marshall said. "Someone would set up on a bale of hay and start pounding away, and my father would record him on a wire recorder," a primitive portable. They met with local distributors, convincing them to carry the newest records, or else trying to get paid. Leonard had to pay the record pressers and recording studios in advance but was himself paid by distributors only when the records sold. This left a gap, an interval of weeks or months when Leonard was exposed, having paid out in cost but yet to recoup in sales. Even if he convinced distributors to carry his record, it meant nothing if the records did not sell. They would just come back as returns. What to the outsider might appear a terrific success might, in fact, be a terrible loss. If Chess sold twenty thousand copies of a record, for example, but pressed sixty thousand, the record would make the charts, but the label still would lose thousands of dollars. Colossal failures came to be known as "platinum returns." "We kept hundreds, thousands of records in our trunk," Marshall told me. "If we ran out, my uncle sent more by bus. My father was building distribution. It was the beginning of the independent record industry."

NOW AND THEN, Leonard would leave Marshall in a hotel room and race into the night, to diners and bars where he met fellow travelers, like-minded men who had started their own labels, makeshift companies run out of houses and storefronts. Many started as vanity presses: for a few dollars, a yokel could record a greeting for his friend in the army, a song for his sweetheart. These labels were nets spread against a great tide; it figured that, over time, genuine talent came up with the haul, dolphins among the carp. But even if the owner of such a label stumbled across a gem and made a record, he probably lacked the know-how, or ambition, or desire to do much with it. The record would at best be sold at the local pharmacy or at the homecoming dance. It might turn up on local radio, which is how, if the planets were aligned, Leonard would hear it floating across the fields. He would ask about it at the station. A phone number would be passed along. Leonard would then sit with the owner of the label, working out the terms: Chess would distribute and sell the record around the country, in return sharing profits. If an artist outgrew his label, Leonard might buy the contract outright.

Leonard had relationships with several independent record men in the South, but none was more important than his friendship with Sam Phillips, who, in the 1950s, founded Sun Records in Memphis. In the history of modern music, Phillips is one of the icons, a founding father who stands at the fork where Rock & Roll diverges from the Blues: Brigham Young coming into the valley of the Great Salt Lake, announcing, "This is the place." Phillips, too, started as a vanity press, but from the beginning wanted to capture the rough music filling the joints on Beal Street. He was among the first record men to sense a white market for race records. He knew the only real obstacle was the color of the musicians. As Robert Junior Lockwood said in *Deep Blues,* "White people down there always did like the Blues. They just didn't like the people who created the Blues." For Phillips, the grail was a white performer who could sing black music. It was this ability, to sing with the voice of another people, that he recognized in Elvis Presley, who, when he was nineteen, a truck driver and a hick, came into the Sun studio to record a birthday song for his mother. Phillips spent hours with Elvis, trying to nail the sound. In the end, it came in a toss-off Presley sang when he thought no one was paying attention—a quick, ragged version of Arthur "Big Boy" Crudup's "That's All Right, Mama."

When the record first aired in Memphis, the station was flooded with calls. The DJ played it again and again. It was not like the work of a cover band: it was familiar yet new, strange. A white singer like Elvis, though he grew up in Tupelo, Mississippi, though he lived near and sang with and prayed beside black people all his life, was, in the end, still just a white boy from the sticks, and so, it was believed, could never really know the lived experience of blacks, could never really sing the Blues. He corrupted the old music with the flavor of his own experience. By trying for a faithful imitation, he invented something new—a hybrid, a mutt, not electric, not diesel, not black, not white, just American. Rock & Roll. This would be the great secret from Dylan to Beck, a brilliant songwriter who is something like Dylan come again—it was those who tried at first to imitate and in the process displayed a transparent longing who would reinvent the old forms. Of course, this sounds like bullshit to those who believe the Blues can be sung only by blacks: that soul, with a capital S, comes from suffering—a communal suffering that is a precursor to the music. "The materials of blues are not available to white Americans," writes LeRoi Jones in *Blues People*. "It's as if these materials are secret and obscure, and blues a kind of ethno-historic rite as basic as blood."

When Elvis broke, Phillips sold his contract to RCA Records

for thirty thousand dollars, the most ever paid for a record deal:
this marks the moment the majors at last took note of the fringe
experiment being conducted by men like Leonard. Once the existence of a market has been proven, the majors get into the game.
Or as Julie Rifkin had told me, "They follow, and when they follow, watch out, because they follow with money." To me, Phillips
is less interesting than Leonard: because he sold the big contract, because he took the easy money, because he made a decision that was small-time and it was a decision that initiated the
terrible transition of Elvis from wild leering figure into declawed
matinee idol. It was a failure of confidence, nerve, imagination.
Leonard would never have sold that contract; he would have
shouted, "All right, motherfuckers! Let's get rich!"

A few years before, Chess and Phillips had gotten into an argument that ruined everything, a seemingly random fight that was
a bad break for Leonard. Had they not fallen out, so Phillips
would later suggest, he might have sold the Elvis Presley contract to Chess. And so: the missed opportunity, the lost ticket to
the big time. And yet, it was not so random after all. The fight
was in fact a classic case of Leonard being Leonard: Sam Phillips
had sold Chess the rights to the Ike Turner song, "Rocket 88."
While on tour to promote the record, which reached the top of
the R&B charts, Turner sent Leonard a bill for a bus ticket.
Leonard sent the bill to Phillips. It turned into a big fight. In the
end, Phillips paid the ticket, Leonard saved a few dollars, and
Elvis Presley went to RCA Records. Character is destiny.

On some trips, Leonard traveled with another record man,
Jerry Blaine from Jubilee, say, two Jews from up North, blasting

from town to town, turning some diner into an oasis of the West Side of Chicago—coffee cups, maps, checklists. Or else he traveled with one of his artists, black man and Jew cruising through the South. This way, Leonard could bring the act to meet distributors and store owners and DJs. You introduce an artist to a distributor, you change him from an abstraction, a voice on a record, into a real human being—it's harder to say no to a real human being.

Leonard made this trip with Muddy, the original Blues singer and the original record man bouncing through Gulfport, Monroe, Alexandria. You had to admire these tidy towns, each with its main street of banks and drugstores, the train station, the tracks dreaming of elsewhere. In the Delta, the air humid, each man with his hair—and kinky hair is where blacks and Jews become one race—blown up like Jiffy Pop, the windshield a paste of dead bugs. In some areas—the gates of a certain neighborhood, the entrance of a certain restaurant—the black artist had to be left behind. "I can tell stories and so can every other man my age in this business," said Bob Krasnow. "I remember traveling with James Brown in New Orleans, and we get to this one street in a cab, and one of us has to get out. And we don't stay in the same hotels. And we don't eat in the same restaurants. And we're not talking 1919. We're talking 1964. The social fabric was fucked, and it absolutely humiliated everyone who touched it."

It was the story of segregation, which, in the mind of my generation, is seen as an exhibit in a museum: black-and-white photographs, a drinking fountain beneath the word COLORED, a mob of white men with axe handles. In these years, a partnership was formed between the Jewish record men and black musicians. It might've been an unbalanced partnership, in that most of the power was on the side of the white businessmen, who tended to see themselves in the role of harsh and stingy but ultimately caring parent. And still, at a time when few Americans took sides, it was a relationship, dysfunctional but real, that would carry on for years, that would blossom in the civil rights moment, the tattered remnants of which can be seen even now at rallies and on public-access television. For Leonard, with his own memories of persecution, these trips into the South came as a shock of recognition. He began donating to the ACLU and the NAACP. Did he give because he really believed, or was it simply guilt money, a payoff for all those artists he bilked? As with many acts of decency, it was probably some of both: high-mindedness mixed with realpolitick is how good things get done in this world.

The crucial task on such trips was visiting radio stations, meeting and greasing the small-town DJs who actually make or break a record. Leonard would park in front of some shoe box of a building in the middle of nowhere, grab a few records, and head into the studio. The DJ says, *Look who just walked in! Leonard from Chess Records in Chicago!* Leonard leans into the microphone, talks about how much he loves this town, the people, the food, then promotes the latest from his label. On the way out, he asks the DJ about his wife and family, then slips him a record with a fifty-dollar bill tucked smartly in the sleeve.

Early on, Leonard realized radio was key. "Disk jockeys wouldn't play your records unless you straightened them out," said Hy Weiss. "There were all sorts of ways. Mostly, you took care of them, were friendly with them." For Leonard, these payoffs were just another expense, a write-off, the cost of doing business. He came to look at his contacts in the radio business almost as employees. On one occasion, he was with friends listening to Stan Lewis, a DJ in Shreveport, Louisiana, saying things like, *You're gonna hear plenty from Chess. Stan is one of my key guys.* An hour into the show, Stan had yet to play a single Chess side. Leonard got Lewis on the phone and really let him have it. Lewis's response came in a letter—a copy was later acquired by Nadine Cohodas and published in her *Spinning Blues into Gold*—that said everything about the weird charisma of Leonard:

> Dear Leonard,
> I have tried in every way to give you all the air play I possibly could. But when you called and bawled me out I knew you were hurt and I don't blame you. But at the same time I was innocent and you hurt me so bad that I cried like a baby. I wish that incident would never had happened as I never wanted you to lose trust in me. If I should die before you, I want you to be one of my pallbearers.

"The Chess guys started beating the shit out of the majors because (a) they'd pay off disc jockeys, (b) they cut deals with record stores," Joe Smith told me. "So yes, these guys were hustlers, they found the talent, they produced the records, they went out and promoted them, they called the distributors to sell them. They were everything. It was the most exciting period in the industry—the independents were just booming."

This was the underbelly of the record business that came to light in the 1950s, with the payola scandal. The government, in the form of the Federal Trade Commission and with that occasional and so astonishingly voracious appetite of less-than-glamorous federal agencies for headlines, declared war on the record man's practice of greasing DJs—which, in a general sense, is legions of dark men gangstering up the airwaves and, in a particular sense, is Leonard Chess taking a twenty-year-old disc jockey out for a steak. This was the era of the quiz-show scandals, the Kefauver hearings on organized crime, Joe McCarthy's hearing on un-American activities. All of it was fueled by a very native paranoia, a sense that the details of life are in fact being controlled by a cabal of men with foreign-sounding names. Which is not to say there is nothing wrong with payola: corrupting the airwaves is as bad as any other form of corruption, though it was not technically illegal. It had in fact been going on for years. But when it was Leonard paying a DJ to spin a race record for a black audience, no one cared; it was just another case of black-on-black crime. It was only when that same record was being played to white kids—when it became Rock & Roll—that it was seen as dangerous. It was not the corruption the government despised. It was the music. Payola. It was like getting Capone on tax evasion.

Payola came to mean Alan Freed, the most popular DJ in America, the "King of Rock & Roll," a man who, in breaking dozens of hits, had taken thousands of dollars from machers like Leonard Chess. Freed actually coined the term Rock & Roll:

Alan Freed (left), the Rock & Roll dj who became the focus of the payola scandal, emerging with his lawyer from court, the worst place for a record man. (© Bettmann/Corbis)

well, not coined so much as moved it from one context to another. For years, in the black community, *rock and roll* had been slang for fucking. *Let's rock and roll all night.* It appeared on race records as early as the 1920s. In the 1922 song by Trixie Smith, "My

Daddy Rocks Me." In the 1951 song by the Dominoes, "Sixty Minute Man": "They call me loving Dan, I rock and roll 'em all night long, I'm the sixty minute man." In 1954, on his radio show in Cleveland, Freed began applying the term to the juiced-up R&B that was coming out of Chicago and Memphis and Detroit. Rock & Roll. It was an inside joke, because the music was low-down and raunchy. Freed moved on to a bigger show in New York in 1956. Then he went national on WCBS. In 1957, he hosted a Rock & Roll television show on ABC. Southern affiliates cut the feed when singer Frankie Lymon ("Why Do Fools Fall in Love?") danced with a white girl. In those years, Freed was followed by wannabe musicians. If he liked a group, he would steer them to Chess or Atlantic or one of the other independents. Leonard would sometimes credit Freed as the co-writer on a song. The actual writer might take offense, but to Leonard it was just smart business: give Freed a monetary interest in a record, you guarantee its success.

The Chess Brothers encouraged and paid and helped Freed to such an extent that they felt a proprietary interest: they thought about him the way gangsters think about politicians they claim to have put in office. There were regular perk-me-ups and loans. Each Christmas, according to Nadine Cohodas, Freed received a lavish gift from the family; for Freed's wedding anniversary, Phil sent a complete set of Baccarat crystal; angry that Freed had not been playing enough of his records, Leonard shouted, "You motherfucker! I pay the mortgage up in goddamned Connecticut!" As the FTC found out, Leonard was paying Freed a hundred dollars a week, a grand sum in those years. Freed said he had taken this money from Chess, and from many other labels, for services rendered. He called himself a consultant. By 1962, as a result of the scandal, Freed's career was in ruins. He pled guilty to two counts of commercial bribery and paid a fine: three hundred dollars. He was dropped by his station; he lost those "consulting" gigs. He wandered off, fell into a stupor, went from small-town gig to small-town gig. His friends were like their records: no play, no pay. In 1965, he died of cirrhosis of the liver. He was forty-two.

Leonard's big fear was being hauled before the FTC and forced to testify—part of a rogues' gallery of record men explaining the life they had made in America. In the end, he was saved by his doggedness. As I said, there is nothing illegal about payola. The fact that the payments were made off the books is how these guys were nailed. Tax evasion. But Leonard, not wanting to lose the exemption, entered each payoff in his books. A business expense, declared and deducted. No case against him was ever made.

Leonard had his first heart attack in 1956. He was forty. In the ensuing years, though he was tough and never compromised his activities—he was the sort of man who lived by the Groucho Marx maxim "Never complain, never explain"—there was a sense of fragility about him. This was before bypass surgery, the incision and quick fix that has allowed so many of our Leonards to continue on with their takeovers and scams and tantrums, and so changed history. For example, had Leonard, who was buying up radio and TV stations at the end, lived into the 1990s, he might well have become a sort of liberal Rupert Murdoch. He instead spent two weeks in the hospital, was urged to consider a

turn in balmier climes—perhaps Miami Beach, the true promised land of the Jews—and was sent home with a prescription
for nitroglycerine and the advice *Just try to take it easy, Leonard.*
In the coming years, his heart would take him in and out of the
hospital. It was in the course of one such visit that Leonard,
asked by a nephew why, when he had accomplished so much
and was already quite wealthy, he continued to strive, spoke the
words that best get at his soul. "It's not the money," he said. "It's
the game."

At the time, Chess Records was grossing around three million
dollars a year, which made it the second most lucrative independent. Atlantic Records took in around six million. Leonard
had already moved the company to 2120 South Michigan Avenue,
where it would spend its most profitable years. He lived in the
office, or across the street at Deutsche's, a diner where deals
were worked out over the house specials, beet borscht, blintzes,
chowder. Leonard had moved his family, wife and three children,
to Glencoe, thirty miles up the lake from Chicago. Tudor man-
sions and ranch houses, leafy streets leading to the lake, which,
this far north, is as clean as a river in Michigan, every pebble
and rock sharp and clear. In the distance, like an explosion without noise, or the details of someone else's life, is the skyline of
the city. To be a Jew in such a town, especially a Jewy Jewstein
like Leonard, must've been funny and irritating and weird but
basically okay. When an artist like Howlin' Wolf came to visit, he
must have been stopped by every cop.

Phil moved to Highland Park, the next town north but a world
away. It was a North Shore equivalent of West End Avenue, in

Manhattan, which had been built as a Jewish alternative to exclusive Park Avenue. Even now, Highland Park feels like a town that fell asleep in Long Island and woke up in the sticks: *what the hell?* There is baked salmon in the stores and good Chinese food and bagels, but of course, like the records made by Chess, bagels have pretty much gone everywhere. When Chuck Berry signed with the label, he would sometimes spend the night with Phil and his family, sharing a room with Phil's son, Terry. Chuck, not wanting to disturb his conked hair, wore a nylon stocking on his head. It sent Terry into fits. Then everyone was laughing, and Chuck swiveled on the balls of his feet, bent his knees, and cruised along the carpet in his fabulous, crowd-pleasing duck-walk. It's good to be the son of a record man!

In these years, Chess reached its peak, with hits and money rolling in, with Leonard signing dozens of artists, cornering the market on Blues, but also recording Soul and Gospel, preachers and Jazz and comedians, whatever the (black) public had a taste for. His roster reads like a history of modern pop: Muddy Waters and Howlin' Wolf and Jimmy Rogers and Little Walter; and later, Bo Diddley, Chuck Berry, Elmore James, Sonny Boy Williamson, Clarence Gatemouth Brown, Koko Taylor, Buddy Guy, Otis Rush, John Lee Hooker, Robert Nighthawk, Billy Boy Arnold; and doo-wop bands like the Flamingos and the Moonglows, led by the great Ben E. King; and Jazz artists like Ahmad Jamal and Ramsey Lewis, and crooners like Dale Hawkins, Etta James, Billy Stewart, Fontella Bass, Rufus Thomas, Dr. Isaiah Ross, Joe Hill Louis, Bobby Bland, Memphis Slim, Eddie Boyd, and Willie Mabon, and old-timers like Big Bill Broonzy and Washboard Sam, and

Howlin' Wolf, 1973. (© Jeff Albertson/Corbis)

comedy albums, and sermons by C. L. Franklin of New Bethel Baptist Church, whose daughter was Aretha Franklin.

For Chess, the key player in this was Willie Dixon, who, as much as Leonard or Phil, came to be the public face of the label. Dixon, a musician and a singer, wrote many of the songs recorded by the company, worked with artists, produced the sessions. A sharp, zeitgeist-directed genius who harbored a smoldering resentment; whatever luck befell him always seemed to befall him a season too late. As a friend of mine said about someone else, "He had a mad-on for the world." Even after decades in Chicago, he looked like he had never left the Delta: big grin, big gut, big laugh, everything oversized. In a bar, he gathered drinks and women, baggy pants and too small jacket Frankenstein-ing up his arms. He took Marshall on drives through the city, bouncing over potholes, floating through traffic lights, talking about the Blues, turning up the radio, explaining the way each beat fell: *You see, all this music comes from slave days. It is the music of the imprisoned Negro. It is three chords, this music, and those three chords come from the three-beat cadence of the field slaves hollering across those fields. So you see, it is really the black man's music, it was made out of his trials and tribulations, and so, ahem, and don't take this wrong, little Chess, but no white man can make this music because no white man has lived it.*

Dixon emigrated from Mississippi in 1936 and settled in the slum, splitting time between his great passions: the stage and the ring. He looked like a big kid, a giant two-year-old, waves and ripples and mountain ranges of fat. He played bass in a group called the Five Breezes. In 1938, as an amateur, he won the Illinois Golden Gloves. When America entered World War II, he refused induction. He said, "Why should I fight to save somebody that's killing me and my people?" He spent ten months in jail. It was the end of his boxing career; in this, Dixon anticipates Mohammed Ali by twenty years.

Even so, he became a fixture on the Blues scene. In the early 1950s, he took a full-time job with Chess. He stayed with the company for years, sometimes fleeing for a better offer, always complaining, but always coming back—Leonard was shit but those other bastards were even worse. He was to become both the most vocal critic of Chess and also the most important protector of its legacy. Some of Dixon's last words on this earth were bad words about Leonard Chess. He said Leonard never paid what was owed, and what he did pay had to be dragged out of him. "I did everything [at the label] from packing records to sweeping floors to answering telephones. They promised to give me so much against royalties, and every week I'd have to damn near fight or beg for the money."

Yet it was Willie Dixon who, when the building at 2120 South Michigan Avenue was condemned, bought it and turned it into a museum which, at every turn, gives credit to Leonard. When a museumgoer asked why so much attention was given the white record man, Dixon explained that, though Leonard was a cheap, chiseling son-of-a-bitch, none of it would have happened without him. Dixon acted as an A&R man for the label, scouting, working with artists, producing sessions, writing songs. Judged by his own records—he released over twenty sides—Dixon might seem a good but not great player, just another name on the roster, but, in fact, in those years, his breath was in everything that came out of Chess. He had an amazing ability to get into the head of a singer and to write for that singer a song the singer should, but could not, write for himself—a song that crystallized a style, a personality, a struggle. The city was in all these tunes, the roar and the energy of it, the way, on a car trip, the engine lurks beneath voices in conversation. For Little Walter, Dixon wrote "My Babe." For Howlin' Wolf, he wrote "Back Door Man." Most significantly, he wrote "Hoochie Coochie Man" for Muddy Waters, which is probably the defining song of the era. "Hoochie Coochie Man" leads like a traffic arrow from 1954 to 1964—from the electric Blues to Rock & Roll.

Dixon taught Muddy the song during a break at the Club Zanzibar. As soon as Muddy had it memorized, he went back out and played the song. With each verse, the crowd got rowdier. By the end, people were standing on their chairs.

Gypsy woman told my mother, before I was born
You got a boy-child comin', gonna be a son-of-a-gun
Gonna make pretty women, jump and shout
And the world will know, what it's all about

Y'know I'm here
Everybody knows I'm here
I'm the hoochie coochie man
Everybody knows I'm here

On the seventh hour, of the seventh day
On the seventh month, the seventh doctor said
"He's born for good luck, and I know you see"
I got seven hundred dollars, don't you mess with me

I got a black cat bone, I got a mojo too
I got the John the Conqueror root, I'm gonna mess with you
I'm gonna make you, pretty girl, lead me by the hand
Then the world will know, I'm the hoochie coochie man

Muddy played the song several times that night. A few weeks later, on January 7, 1954, he recorded it for Leonard. Within months, it had become Muddy's anthem the way "My Way," with lyrics written by Paul Anka, would become the anthem of Frank Sinatra. It's driving beat became the most familiar thing about the electric Blues, a sound that swirls around the legacy like scraps of paper that swirl around the spot from which Superman ascended. Of course, the success of the song was really all about Willie Dixon, how he could shape a song to a particular voice. The imagery, the boasting, the gypsy woman—these were Dixon's trademarks. "In the South, gypsies would come around and tell fortunes," he later explained. "When I was a little boy, you'd see a covered wagon coming and these women with their great big dresses—dog-gone knows how many dresses they'd have on— and pockets up under them." The voodoo, the mojo, the black cat bone, the John the Conqueror root—all of it plays on the old Robert Johnson idea of a devilish presence. And that weird, poetic specificity—the seventh hour, the seventh doctor, the seven hundred doctors, the seventh son—which gives the music its tremendous mystery and power. "The seventh son is a historical idea," said Dixon. "In Algiers in Louisiana they have people who they say are born for good luck because they're the seventh sister or seventh brother or seventh child." This specificity sounds like numerology or witchcraft, the casting of a spell that remains unbroken. Bob Dylan has spoken of coming across "Hoochie Coochie Man" on the radio late one night in his parents' house, in Hibbing, Minnesota. A low ceiling of clouds had bounced the signal clear from Chicago: Muddy Waters, like a voice from another world:

On the seventh hour, of the seventh day
On the seventh month, the seventh doctor said
"He was born for good luck, and I know you will see
I got seven hundred dollars, don't you mess with me

It was a transcendent moment for young Bob, and his song-writing never got over it. His best work still carries its echo, that strange particularity that hints at a great big secret, which is a fake—well, not a fake, but not his secret; nor is it, as has been argued in all sorts of books, a secret from the King James Bible, or the Romantic poets, or the Beats. It is, in fact, the secret of Willie Dixon riding his groove at 2120 South Michigan Avenue. Bob Dylan is Willie Dixon run through a radio, then through the brain of an especially clever, ambitious white kid in the suburbs.

Here is young Bob on "Highway 61 Revisited":

Now the fifth daughter on the twelfth night
Told the first father that things weren't right
My complexion, she said, is much too white
He said, Come here and step into the light, he says, hmm,
  you're right
Let me tell the second mother this has been done
But the second mother was with the seventh son
And they were both out on Highway 61

What do you call an homage that fans do not recognize as an homage, that instead reaches them as strange and new, an entirely original discovery?

Over the years, Willie Dixon, who did his best work at Chess, grew disillusioned with the label, then angry, then became its most vocal critic. Dixon's autobiography, *I Am the Blues,* is a howl at the center of a debate that has raged for years: *was that first generation of record men good and necessary and constructive, or were they manipulative and evil?* In Willie Dixon's eyes, we see Leonard Chess the shtarker, the shyster, the hoodwinker, the chiseler. Leonard was, in fact, far less complicated. Simply put, he was a scrapper. He'd been struggling all his life, and for him the world was a battlefield, a war against the elements and fates, and getting rich did not change that. Even when he made it, he still fought for pennies. On one occasion, Leonard almost came to blows with Big Boy Crudup, who, at the start of a session, said he would not sing without whiskey. Leonard bought a bottle, then, at the end of the session, when Crudup was loaded, deducted it from the singer's fee. "Most of these musicians were paid scale," said Dixon. "The union required the musicians be paid within fourteen days of the session, but most wanted their money the day they finished. Leonard would say, 'If you take half the money, I'll give it to you now.'"

"He was a maneuverer," said Dixon. "He was dealing with people who didn't know anything about the business. Some people call it smart. I call it swindling when you take advantage of someone who don't know no better."

In these years, Leonard did in fact play close to the line, running a kind of street game that manipulated the personality, the vanity, the pride of each artist. If you were a singer who needed love or praise, or if you were dim-witted or hotheaded, you were going to get screwed. It was show business: the girls want to fuck the singer—that is why most of them got on stage in the first place—and so do the record companies. It had less to do with race than with profit. In interview after interview, record men told me some version of the old chestnut: "The only color I care about is green."

For Leonard, it was a process, a ritual as time-tested and thrilling as the one-night stand. It meant getting a scouting report from Willie Dixon or spotting an artist through the smoke of some dive, then cornering the act backstage, showering him with praise, giving him a glimpse of a future as neat and serene as a diorama—Big Boy in a mansion, a Cadillac in the driveway, gardeners on the lawn. *Follow me, it's yours.* Meeting the next day at 2120 South Michigan, small talk and drinks, and a contract is pushed across the desk. *It seems fast, but we really want to get you into the studio.*

Only later does the artist realize he has signed away every right, a contract filled with small type and trapdoors; conveniently, it seems, no copies of the actual documents survive. All the riders and clauses have faded like invisible ink, leaving Leonard laughing at the crossroads. Most maddening were the publishing rights, gone like dust in that tune by Kansas—"Dust in the Wind," it's called—signed over to Leonard, who, along with Gene and Harry Goodman, the brothers of the big-band leader Benny Goodman, formed a company called Arc Publishing. Whenever a singer recorded a song already released by Chess, the royalty went not to the act who performed the original but to Arc Publishing, a side venture that paid in dribs and drabs before

Elvis, and in great torrents after, when the major labels started signing white kids to cover every Blues classic. Wolf or Sonny Boy might complain, *I'm getting fucked,* and Leonard might commiserate, *Yes, it's an ugly world,* as he cleaned up on the publishing rights. He was like one of the great trading houses of Wall Street. He won even when his artists lost.

If pressed, Leonard, and the other executives of that era, would claim the real money was not in records anyway. It was in the live dates that came as a result of those records. "The value for an artist was to enhance bookings and fees on the road," Hy Weiss told me. For example, Willie Mabon, who made twenty dollars a gig before he met Leonard, was, after his records were released, making two hundred—which is, of course, entirely beside the point.

After Leonard died, a lawyer named Scott Cameron filed suits on behalf of Dixon and Waters, claiming Chess tricked some artists into signing wildly inappropriate deals. "There is a little-known portion of copyright law called 'Employee For Hire,' which is generally used in a film or if you're scoring something for a play," he is quoted as saying in Dixon's *I Am the Blues.* "A music publisher hires a writer to write a specific score. The writer is paid a salary and then the publishing company, and not the writer, owns the rights to that song. I found that Muddy and Willie, without comprehending, signed those kinds of agreements. Muddy signed his for two thousand dollars. It was retroactive back to the fifties. It meant that when he died his family would not have the right to any income derived from the copyrights."

(Other independents had even harsher contracts. One old-timer told me he "fucked" every woman singer he recorded. Asked how he did it, he said, "You put it in the contract.")

Unlike many early record men, Leonard did not actually cross the line. His practices, though manipulative and tricky, were never illegal. It was a question merely of finding the loop hole, or the tick clause, the legal advantage. As Ron Malo said, *Leonard screwed them honest.* This meant atrocious royalty deals. Whereas a major might pay an artist five or six cents when a record sold, a Chess artist was paid two or three cents. "It was shit," said Bob Krasnow. "Two or 3 percent of the profits. Maybe Sinatra was only getting 6 percent, but these guys were still getting only 50 percent of what everyone else was getting."

"I don't know of any overt ripping off," Marshall Chess told me. "Yes, we paid low royalties, but so did everyone else. I used to see my father go through statements, and all I ever saw him do was, once, take money from one artist and give it to another who needed the money to live." (Note: Leonard played redistributor not with his own wealth but with the wealth of another artist. Whenever I hear Leonard given this spin, I think of Mel Brooks as *The 2000 Year Old Man* debunking Robin Hood: "He took from everyone and kept everything.")

"All independents of that era treated artists in the same way," Marshall added. "A guy comes to you, he wants to sell you this, he needs the money. It's called business."

Leonard worked it so that royalties were paid only after he recovered all his expenses, and since only Leonard knew just how much a session had cost, or what other expenses might have gone into a release, and since he did not open his books, an artist, even an artist with a hit, might never get paid. Or Leonard might say, *Yes, lots of records were shipped, but we're expecting lots of returns.*

When Dick Lapalm, an executive at Chess, hit with "Blues Heaven," which he co-wrote with Willie Dixon—it was the B side of "Wang Dang Doodle," which sold around 200,000 copies— he received a check for sixteen dollars. When he complained, Phil Chess said, "You can buy yourself a good breakfast."

Joe Smith, who, in his early years, managed a few bands, sent the Tune Weavers to Chess, where they hit with "Happy Birthday Baby." "When I got the royalty report, I couldn't believe it," Smith told me. "Leonard said, 'Oh, Christ, Joe, we just normally knock 35 percent off everything.'" Smith then said, "A publisher named George Pincus sent the accountant at Mercury Records a case of 150-watt lightbulbs because, he said, the light in the accounting department apparently wasn't sufficient to read the sales figures."

For his record *I Don't Know,* which sold a hundred thousand copies, Willie Mabon received a royalty check for thirty-seven hundred dollars. As legend has it, he went down to the office with a gun—you might be surprised by just how many singers went to Chess or Atlantic or Mercury with a weapon of some kind. Leonard took Mabon by the arm, filled him with mumbo-jumbo, paid his back rent and then, at Christmas, sent him a fruit basket.

To singers and songwriters, the company was "Plantation Chess." Leonard was the master and the sole occupant of the big house. (Again, I say this with all due respect to Phil.) Artists who had grown up in the South seemed only too willing to fall into the role. "I thought Leonard was the best man in the business," Muddy Waters told a newspaper reporter. "He did a lot for me. I didn't even sign no contract. It was just, 'I belongs to the Chess family.'" Life at the label has been compared to share-cropping. Artists were often paid not in cash but in goods and services, in credit in the company store. These goods were given as if they were gifts, and then later, to the shock of the recipients, subtracted from royalties. An artist who spent several years with Leonard might find, when he decided to leave, that he actually owed money to the label. "If in all the time I was with Chess he gave me 75 thousand dollars, I will eat my hat," Bo Diddley told *Rolling Stone*. "When I left, they said I owed them 125 grand."

"That generation was terribly paternal," said Bob Krasnow. "James Brown would come off the road, and Syd Nathan at King Records would buy him a bunch of clothes, a Cadillac, a case of wine and send him home to take a couple of weeks off. Then charge it to his royalties. Remember, Leonard and his brother, and Marshall and those guys, only made black music. Syd Nathan only made black music, and Brunswick, and Atlantic. So what was the morality of this setup? Was a Cadillac given instead of what should have been given? What did Chess really get from his artists, and what did those artists really get from Chess?"

To hear Marshall and Leonard and Phil tell it, the artists got quite a lot. For starters, it was only guys like Leonard who would record guys like Muddy and Wolf. And so they are now defamed for being the only white Americans willing to get into that particular game. And yes, Sinatra got a better deal, but a hit by Sinatra meant two million copies, whereas a hit by Little Walter meant thirty thousand copies. Leonard could not pay as well because

Leonard's artists did not sell nearly as many records. In the world of independents, all the margins were small. A single mistake could wreck a company. And since only one out of every six or seven releases made any noise, the hits had to pay for the duds. Sonny Boy Williamson might bitch if Leonard did not pay promptly when a record hit, but he never said a word when Leonard spent twenty grand on a Sonny Boy record that tanked. As for the matter of royalties, yes, money was deducted, which might, to an artist with a hit, make it seem like he wasn't getting paid, but maybe he should've thought of that when he demanded cash to pay a gambling debt or buy a car. "They came in whenever they had a problem," Phil Chess is quoted as saying in *Spinning Blues into Gold*. "If one had his wife having a baby in one hospital and his old lady in another, he would come to us to pay for the old lady so the wife wouldn't find out. That was an advance on royalties. But he would forget." In 1970, when Muddy, who never thought to buy insurance, wrecked his Cadillac and spent over two months in the hospital, Leonard paid the bill. When Muddy got loaded on whiskey in Tuscaloosa, Alabama, and was arrested for driving drunk, Leonard paid the ticket. If such payoffs had been considered gifts, Chess would have gone out of business in the early fifties.

The style of Plantation Chess is often justified with the story of Etta James, a saloon singer who struggled for years before her boyfriend, Bobby Lester of the Moonglows, sent her to Leonard. "The brothers are some smart Jews who know how to sell records," he said. Her first hit was "At Last." She went on to record many more, including "Tomorrow Night," "All I Could Do Was Cry,"

Phil again, hovering over Etta James, who made great music, but needed hovering over. (Michael Ochs Archives.com)

and "Don't Go to Strangers." There is something creepy and strung out and authentically desperate about all these songs, and in fact James was a terrific junky. Now and then, Leonard had to bail her out of jail. On the ride home, the city wandering past the windows, so cold and lonely in the middle of the night, he would say, *Come on, Etta, you've got a real gift. Get your shit together.* In the studio, he would shout, *Sing it, mother.* When she broke down in tears—she was a fantastic drugged-out crying machine—he would say, *Use it in the music, baby.* He refused to pay many of the royalties she was owed, saying it would only feed her habit. Instead, he used the money to buy her a house. She was furious at the time but later said it was only the house that kept her alive. "Even when I lost everything, Leonard made sure I had somewhere to live."

In other words, Leonard had with his artists the sort of relationship that, no matter how well meaning, breeds resentment. "You hear it all the time [from the artists]," Phil Spector told *Rolling Stone*. " 'We bought your house and don't forget it, boy. You're livin' in the mansion our songs paid for and driving the Cadillac we got. You stole it from us.' "

Later, when the industry was overtaken by corporations, some of these artists would change their opinion. They had worked so closely with Leonard they could smell his breath and his stink, the insult and will of another human being. The corporations played the same game, only better and smoother and fiercer, picking clean every bone but leaving behind no prints, no evidence, no anecdotes, nothing to hold or hate, just an empty room where your song, or a pirated version of it ("Revolution" by the Beatles), plays on a Nike commercial, credited to another singer.

5

The Kids Dig It,
but the Kids Are Sick

B y the midfifties, Chess Records had become its own world, a messy little universe of artists and engineers and promo men and feuds, and as such it had developed its own energy, a tremendous pull that drew talent from across the South and Midwest. In 1955, Chuck Berry, just a few years out of high school, traveled from St. Louis to Chicago to see his hero, Muddy Waters, perform. It was a hinge moment, the future visiting the past, the boy prince seeking the blessing of the soon-to-be-deposed king. In the years since World War II, a nation of kids had come of age, teenagers, a baggy term that would come to identify those millions locked in the fierce process of becoming, stranded in the no-man's-land between the world of their parents and a world of their own; a nation without music or culture. To those who could read the signals, this was a moment experienced as a climb in the barometer. The Blues and R&B had become increasingly poppy—lighter and brighter and strung with jinglelike melodies you just can't shake—in response to the

growing numbers of white kids in the South who, in the manner of young Bob Dylan, were seeking out Negro radio stations,
plugging into the music of the underclass, turning up at the
dives, the white face that portends trouble. In an essay in
Cashbox, Ahmet Ertegun and Jerry Wexler predicted the trend,
saying the Blues would change to meet the tastes of the bobby
soxers, white kids seeking authentic experience. This new
sound—they called it "cat music"—would be an amped version
of Fats Domino or the Clovers. "Up-to-date blues with a beat,
and infectious catch phrases, and danceable rhythms," wrote
Wexler and Ertegun. "It has to kick and it has to have a message
for the sharp youngsters who dig it."

Chuck Berry was the product of this moment and also its
enabler. He would take the electric Blues and run it through a
blender, through the brand-new teen sensibility—he was just
nineteen and so part of a generation decades younger than Muddy
or Wolf—that would turn his songs into anthems, epics for the
vast in-between: it was the first emergence of a truly suburban
music. In this, he was infinitely more modern than Elvis. What
was modern about Elvis was his color: a white kid singing Delta
Blues. What was modern about Chuck was his sound: a black
kid singing Blues/Pop for the American teen, Chicago remade as
a collection of sharp flashy guitar licks that form the foundation
of every Rock & Roll song that jumps. So it was proper that Chuck
went first to see Muddy, the inventor of the (soon-to-be) old
music.

Chuck was so sharp in those years—well, really, he kept his
look forever, so long that in the late 1970s, in a movie about Alan

Freed called *American Hot Wax,* he played his earlier, 1950s self, convincingly. His face was as geometric as the triangle they make the tone-deaf kid play in band. He wore two-tone shoes, velvet coats, yellow shirts, suede shoes—that whole generation of rockers dressed like Beal Street pimps, or, if they missed the mark—and often they did—like traveling salesmen. Chuck pumped Muddy's hand after the show, saying, *Man, you were really cutting it! I'm your biggest fan! And I play guitar, too! Tell me, man, how can I get a record made?* In a toss-off, over his shoulder, going away, Muddy said, *Go see Leonard over at Chess Records.*

Chuck Berry grew up in St. Louis, a son of the black middle class that emerged after the war. He lived in a world of school dances and car races and the rest of that movie. In wedding the poor city Blues to the passions of the middle class, he would create a new music. Charlie Watts, the drummer of the Rolling Stones, told me, "You know, it's crazy, we get so much acclaim, and all we've done for the last forty years is imitate Chuck Berry." Chuck made his first appearances in high school talent shows, coming on after the comedy routines and juggling acts, his guitar buzzing with feedback, blinking into the cavern of seats, counting off, one, two, three, the room filling with the howl of his Gibson guitar, a new version of one of the old Muddy Waters and Jimmie Rogers tunes; yet, when he played one of these songs, because he had his own sensibility and because he had the temperament of an artist, it was jumpier and wilder and new. Take a Muddy Waters 33 and play it at 45 rpms, and you get a sense of just where Chuck Berry comes from. It's as if some old Blues tune had gotten into the medicine cabinet and swallowed a bunch of Benzedrine. And now it's hopped up, gone on goofballs, running on, riff after riff, as sharp and clear as lake water—as opposed to, say, muddy water. It was the difference between growing up in a Midwestern city and growing up on a plantation in Mississippi.

After high school, Chuck went on a spree—a car-steeling spree, dancing joyride to joyride, racing across the country, chasing that wide-open feeling he captured in songs like "Maybellene": "Cadillac pulled up to hundred and four, Ford got hot and wouldn't do no more, then got cloudy and started to rain, I tooted my horn for the passing lane." He was caught by the police ("I put my foot on my tank and began to roll, moaning siren, 'twas the state patrol"), went to trial, and was sentenced. But it was his first offense and he was brimming with talent, and so was soon released. He took a job as a janitor at a radio station, absorbing every song the jockey played. After work, he practiced with a band. It was terrifically noisy. Cat music. Blues. Rhythm & Blues. Race Music. It was old and not old, and in it you could hear the symbols and obsessions of the country Blues remade with the power and speed of the city. In one song, Chuck plays with the idea of the freight train, the Illinois Central of Son House and Robert Johnson, which reappears like a nightmare symbol, a devil train, the great domino of the fiery north:

As the train rushed on at a terrible pace
Sulfuric fumes scorched their hands and face
Wider and wider the country grew
Faster and faster the engine flew

Louder and louder the thunder crashed
Brighter and brighter the lightin' flashed
Hotter and hotter the air became
Till their clothes were burned with each quivering refrain
Then out of the din there came a yell
Ha ha said the devil we're nearing home

Chuck headed to Chicago, Chi, that great stain of a city, a jumpy jukebox of a town, neighborhoods, with their dagos and kikes and wops and micks and Negroes and Finns and Slavs and Polacks, churches and saloons and music halls and club rooms stitching up the flats like a quilt—unbelievable! You can just walk into a town like that and shake hands with Muddy Waters! And so, early the next morning, Chuck is standing with his guitar in front of Chess Records, kicking and cursing and muttering in the cold, waiting for someone to unlock the door. At last, a tough little man glides up in a Cadillac, parks, walks right past Chuck, hardly seems to notice him, unlocks the door in a jangle of keys, takes in the mail, then, without looking up, says, *All right, kid, you got something to show me, come inside.*

This is the quality that kept Leonard in the game long after most of the old-time record men had bailed: a never-ending willingness to hear the kid from the street. To be impressed, to be amazed. Past forty, most music executives lose patience, discover their fathers were right, and so turn the gut-check decisions over to an army of kids, new eyes, new ears, explaining, to anyone who might ask, *It's a young man's game.* After hearing a demo, such men turn to one of these kids and ask, *Do I like it?* But

Leonard never lost touch with the street, never moved to an office in the Loop. Even in the roughest years of city life, his door was open to anyone who had a new slant on the old script.

Chuck played two, three, five songs. After years of Muddy and Wolf, imagine how this music sounded to Leonard. The rhythm of the train was still there, only now it was a freakin' bullet train. It was a new music with an old mood, and it is natural to ask: Where did Chuck get this music? What were his influences? Much came from the Blues, of course; some say the speed and the drive of his guitar were borrowed from the piano of Otis Spann: it is said Chuck transferred this sound from piano to guitar the way Little Walter transferred the solos of Louis Jordan from the sax to the harmonica. And though there was much Chuck Berry copied and stole, he had, in fact, created something new. Only once in a very great while does someone actually create something new. The rest of us, even the most brilliant, spend our time just working out the implications. Even now, we are still in the moment created by Chuck Berry—at the other side of that moment, maybe, on the distant rim of the soap bubble, but still the same moment. Rock & Roll was invented by Chuck Berry in 1955. And to me, it never sounds better than it does on the first five or ten sides released by Chess.

It was not just the melody—it was the words. He had refashioned the creepy book of the Blues into the bright, hard focus of Rock & Roll. Singers like Neil Young and John Lennon might warp this voice with hallucinogens, or run it through a wah-wah pedal, or reshape it to the causes of the day, but it remained in some essential way the same voice of Chuck Berry—a voice that looked forward to Nick Lowe and Elvis Costello as much as it looked back to Son House and the Mississippi Sheiks. Chuck was a bridge out of the Blues, the ant that lays down its body so the others can cross. He created a sea of phrases that would turn up again and again. Here is a verse from "You Can't Catch Me," written by Berry in 1956:

New Jersey Turnpike in the wee wee hours
I was rollin' slow because of drizzlin' showers
Here come old flat-top, he was movin' up with me
Then come wavin' goodbye a little' old souped-up jitney
I put my foot in my tank and I began to roll
Moanin' siren, 'twas a state patrol.

And here is "Open All Night," written by Bruce Springsteen, in 1984:

Your eyes get itchy in the wee wee hours
Sun's just a red ball risin' over them refinery towers
Radio's jammed up with gospel stations
Lost souls callin' long distance salvation.

As I said, Chuck was both the product and the enabler of this particular moment: the example of his songs encouraged hundreds of musicians to play Rock & Roll. His records, which seemed to have no message at all, were in fact advertisements for a new life, a Rock & Roll culture, what The Who would call "a teenage wasteland" and what Bruce Springsteen would call

*Chuck Berry. In his music, you could still hear the Illinois
Central, only now it was a freakin' bullet train.* (Southern
Folklife Collection, University of North Carolina, Chapel Hill)

"the teenage nation." In trying to chronicle the world of the
American teen, Chuck Berry had created it. For the first time,
with songs like "Roll Over Beethoven" and "Rock & Roll Music,"
the music becomes the singer of its own glory—a movement.
You can draw a straight line from Chuck Berry's "Sweet Little

Sixteen" to the Beach Boys "Surfin USA"—it is in fact the same song—to the Beatles "Let It Be," to Woodstock, and then on to the Real World on MTV. The emergence of Chuck Berry marked the beginning of the end of the old America.

Leonard told Chuck to come back with a demo. The song on the tape that jumped was called "Ida May." No one had ever heard anything like it. But there already was a song called "Ida May" so Leonard told Chuck they needed a new name. As engineers and musicians brainstormed, Leonard noticed a tube of lipstick a girl left behind. "Why don't we call it 'Maybellene'?" It took thirty-seven takes. "You Can't Catch Me" was cut for the B side. At Chess, the first pressing of a single was usually around five thousand copies. If Leonard was confident, he might press ten thousand. The first pressing of "Maybellene" was thirty thousand. Leonard knew this was his chance: this new music, not yet called Rock & Roll, was his way into the mainstream.

In those weeks just before and just after the release, the key moment in the life of any record, Leonard went into a hyperselling mode that no one in the business could match. It's what made him a legend. For starters, he split the writing credit, half to Chuck Berry, half to Alan Freed. In common wisdom, guys like Leonard take for themselves. But here Leonard gives to Freed so Freed will have an interest in the record and so feature it on his radio show. Berry's contract included a clause that kicked 10 percent of the gross back to the company, which Leonard probably used to pay off DJs, record stores, and television producers. When Chuck went on the road, Leonard went with him, greasing the producer, making sure Chuck got top billing. At one show,

Berry argued with Leonard. "It was around '55, '56," Chuck later said. "I was on Dick Clark's show and he wanted me to lip-synch. I refused. I said, 'Chuck Berry is not gonna open his mouth and have nothing come out.' So Leonard came over and we had a talk. I figured if anyone is gonna tell me what to do right, Leonard will. And Leonard says, 'There are some things you got to do in this business that you don't want to do.' "

When "Maybellene" hit, employees of Chess had to stay at the office all night to fill the reorders. It was the biggest score in the history of the label—and amazingly, it was twinned by another huge hit, a Chess release by Ellis McDaniel, who signed with Leonard around the same time. After getting turned down by Vee Jay and United, McDaniel just walked in off the street. He had gone to a Chicago vocational school and built his own guitar, a big square instrument that matched his big square face, big square glasses, and big square hands. His band was called the Langley Avenue Jive Cats. He had two songs on tape, "I'm a Man," modeled on "Hoochie Coochie Man"—he had been sneaking into clubs to see Muddy since he was twelve—and "Uncle John," which featured verses like:

> *Uncle John's got corn ain't never been shucked*
> *Uncle John's got daughters ain't never been . . .*
> *To school.*

Schmuck, you'll never get that song on the radio. Find some new words.

Someone in the band remembered a clown he had seen named

Bo Diddley. And so this became the name of the song, and the name of the performer, and the name of McDaniel's jazzed-up version of the "Hoochie Coochie" drum pattern—the Bo Diddley beat.

"Maybellene" and "Bo Diddley"—these songs outsold the rest of the Chess roster combined. It was a breakthrough. The company had gone from selling tens of thousands to selling hundreds of thousands of records. "And it was more than just the numbers," Marshall told me. "We noticed records selling in places that we never before sold records: New York, Boston, Philly—all over the Northeast, in white neighborhoods, too."

So there you have it: Rock & Roll, the item at the bake sale that gets the notice of the national chain. Too much notice, in fact: for the first time, the company had attracted a competitive interest from the major labels: big game draws big-game hunters.

In the first years of Rock & Roll, interest from the major labels meant cover songs: a white artist hired to sing a watered-down knockoff of a song already scored as a regional hit by a black artist. The mainstream, or so it was reasoned, would more readily accept the new sound from a singer that looked like the audience. I am not talking about the records of Carl Perkins or Roy Orbison or Elvis Presley, who were no less genuine than Chuck or Muddy—*and of course Elvis, with his TV appearances in 1956, and his tremendous power and sexuality, blew the lid off the old construct*—but a legion of pretenders who were recruited the way boy bands are recruited today. These songs were sent up like the first rockets launched by NASA, those you see in old news clips that rise fifty or sixty feet before collapsing in flames. They were a joke the fool takes seriously. In fact, why not start laughing and continue right through the rest of this paragraph, through Pat Boone singing Little Richard's "Tutti Frutti," Ricky Nelson singing Fats Domino's "Ain't That a Shame," Bill Haley singing Big Joe Turner's "Shake, Rattle & Roll." Money was spent on these sessions and the songs were played on the radio and someone must have had a life-affirming moment as Ricky Nelson sang "Ain't That a Shame," and Pat Boone probably walked out of a studio thinking, "I really nailed it," but these songs were an ugly trick played on the American public, faded now like a bland memory, a false lead in a capital case—an insult returned years later when the early punk bands, which were as close in spirit as you get to those first rock bands, covered the Pop standards, like the Sex Pistols doing Sinatra's "My Way." The early covers failed because they were fake. One of the great qualities of a song by Chuck Berry or Elvis Presley is its authenticity—those songs reek of the real. The covers were market-tested nothings, the closest thing I know to Holden Caulfield's definition of the word phony.

And yet their appearance marked the beginning of the end of the independents. With "Maybellene" and "Bo Diddley," Leonard had cracked the piñata, a success that summoned the forces that would destroy him. He had gone into the studio with Chuck Berry in the morning and come out and it was night—the neon night of Rock & Roll, with competition from dozens of labels and singers, whole movements aimed at the newly discovered youth market. It was the moment of Elvis Presley and Carl Perkins and Rockabilly, of great musicians like Eddie Cochran and Buddy Holly, and others not so great. Records would soon cost much more to produce and well-represented white artists were not half as easy to dupe into bad contracts. An early sign came in 1956, when RCA Victor paid Sam Phillips thirty-five grand for Elvis. The table minimum had suddenly been raised to a point where operators like Leonard would be pushed out of their own game. Or maybe they were just finished: by bringing the best of the fringes to the mainstream, maybe these independents, in the manner of third parties in the American political system, had fulfilled their destiny. "The demise was inevitable as soon as the big companies realized this was a hell of a business," Joe Smith told me. "They would start buying up independents, and this little world these guys built would be wiped out. Atlantic, Chess, Motown, Imperial—one by one they would cash out or give way. They were amazing people, but the writing was on the wall."

THIS FIRST MOMENT of Rock & Roll was glory for Leonard and Phil, yet no one really talks about what it meant for the Blues musicians who made it possible. It killed them, of course. It wiped them out. It sent them into early retirement. It tossed them from the theaters into the clubs. It forced them back into the steel mills and packing houses. It moved them from the present tense into the past. It made them colorful characters of the has-been variety. It was like that lyric from my own child-hood, "Video killed the radio star." The backwash of history, the spit that, as anyone who has shared a Coke at camp can tell you, winds up at the bottom of the bottle, the suds that spill off as the machine shifts from spin into rinse, a generation of blues-

men lost in the wash. "Rock & Roll, which Chess helped introduce and popularize by recording Chuck Berry and Bo Diddley,
hit the old delta bluesmen hard," Robert Palmer writes in *Deep
Blues*. "A number of them—Nighthawk, Sonny Boy, Elmore—
went back to the South and performed there when times were
toughest up North. Even Muddy found the going rough, but
maintained his loyal ghetto audience in Chicago."

The marginal players vanished into retirement, into that
nowhere of historical figures who have seen their moment come
and go, where, twenty or thirty years later, they would be "rediscovered" by aficionados—Lonnie Johnson sweeping floors in the
South, Jimmy Rogers working at a slaughterhouse in Chicago.
Muddy and Wolf, and all those of the first rank, would always
have a place in the clubs, but they lost their position at the break
of the wave. Chess would continue to promote and produce their
records: for Muddy, it was the beginning of a long twilight of
reinvention, with producers—especially Marshall, who, after a
brief stint in college, started working for the company full-time
in the midsixties—trying to repackage Muddy as, variously, an
early example of Rock & Roll, the last vintage folky, the father of
every scene. It was in these years that the label began to promote Muddy in Britain, which, free of American noise and prejudice, sometimes picks out what we've missed—the glimmer in
the grass. The English taste for Blues was first noticed at Chess
by increasing requests for live performances and by the growing
numbers of mail-order sales. In 1958, Leonard traveled to
London. He hated it, of course, a typical greenhorn reaction to
anything as old and history-haunted as Europe, the trap left

behind. "He didn't like that whole way of doing things," Marshall told me. "He was one of those kinds of immigrants: new car, new buildings. He wanted everything new." But Leonard never let personal feelings get in the way of business—money is money. He signed a distribution deal with British Decca Records, which, for the first time, would sell Chess sides in England. The revolution was about to be exported.

Muddy Waters made his first trip abroad that same year. With his American sales waning, he went to England in the manner of Frampton going to Japan, a fading star hoping to squeeze one more season out of the senior circuit. This was before those armies of British bands came to America; the idea of an English audience for Blues, let alone of British Blues musicians, was still a wacky figment. The band was met mostly with shock. British critics were expecting a folky relic of old Negro America, field hollers and moans, but instead got a music as strange and threatening as rap was on its first appearance—an absolutely modern sound, a hymn to electricity. Muddy read the reviews, most of them bad. The critics complained about the noise, which made it impossible to weep to the sorrow of it all. Of course, to the kids it was something else. In America, Muddy fathered a generation of rockers who played off his lyricism. In Britain, Muddy fathered a cult of noise: bands that took away the lesson that a big noise is the only way to get across in an era of noise. This philosophical proposition reached its purest expression with The Who, a band that billed itself, possibly in reply to the Rolling Stones, who had been called "The World's Greatest Rock & Roll band," as "The World's Loudest Rock & Roll band." (In 1977, when I was a kid, my brother went to see The Who. The band was on tour for its album *Who's Next,* which, on the cover, showed the band members peeing, or just having peed, on a stone wall. I asked him, "How was it?" And he said, "It was two days ago and my ears are still ringing! Fucking great is how it was!")

Muddy was a muckraker stumping through the slums, shouting, pounding, stirring dissent. What's the phrase? To sow the whirlwind. To the young men, his music was an ideology, a system that would overturn the culture of the day. I am thinking of a sentence in a George Trow essay that reads, "I've seen Mick Jagger dancing on the ashes of western civilization." His music would be remade by a handful of British bands and then returned to American as a driving force. It is what the boys at Intelligence call blowback. It was the 1950s—the era of Muddy Waters and Chuck Berry and Bo Diddley and Elvis Presley—spun into something new. David Bowie's original band was called the Mannish Boys, after the song by Muddy. Mick Jagger and Keith Richards had been playmates as toddlers, but they really got together as adolescents. Keith spotted Mick carrying a stack of Chess records, which Mick had ordered from Chicago. Keith said, *Hey, you like those, too?* Richards told me the original goal of their band had been "to turn other people on to Muddy Waters." Their first hit was "I Just Wanna Make Love to You," a song written for Muddy by Willie Dixon. Their first monster, "I Can't Get No Satisfaction," echoes the early Waters tune, "I Can't Be Satisfied"; in an interview, Jagger said its main phrase came from the Chuck Berry song "Thirty Days," specifically from the line "I can't get no satisfaction from the judge." When the Beatles made their first trip to America in 1964, a reporter asked Paul McCartney what he wanted to see. He said, "Muddy Waters." When the reporter asked, "What is Muddy Waters?" McCartney said, "Don't you even know your famous people in this country?"

On American tours, musicians like McCartney and Jagger would go slumming on the South Side of Chicago. You would see them cutting down a ragged street trailed by reporters. For Brits, seeking out the old bluesman was a way to plug into the authentic, to give back what they stole. Was it Dizzy Gillespie who said, in reference to his own musical influences, "You can't steal a gift"? The Blues "is primitive and no bullshit," John Lennon said in *Rolling Stone*. "It's the beat from the jungle, a simple rhythm that goes throughout the world. Eldridge Cleaver said blacks gave the middle-class whites back their bodies. I believe that." Magic Dick of the Jay Giles band met the Muddy Waters band in Cambridge, Massachusetts, where, trying to act cool, he took aside Otis Spann and showed him a cube of hashish. *Thanks*, said Spann, and popped the entire cube in his mouth. A few days later, Magic Dick, who told the story to Sandra B. Tooze for her book *Muddy Waters: The Mojo Man*, asked Spann how he had liked the drug. Spann said, "I didn't know where I was for a long time." With the help of Marshall, the manager of the Yardbirds, Giorgio Gomelsky, set up a summit between his band and some of the legends of Chess. "I'll never forget it," Gomelsky said in *I Am the Blues*. "It was an afternoon about four o'clock in March of 1964. There was Howlin' Wolf and Sonny Boy and Willie Dixon on this sofa. Willie was huge, Wolf wasn't exactly small, and Sonny Boy was towering and lean. And there are Jimmy Page and

Eric Clapton sitting at their feet. Willie was singing and tapping on back of a chair and Sonny Boy playing harmonica."

Mick Jagger said he got from black musicians, in addition to everything else, a sense that words are not crucial. "I don't think lyrics are that important," he told *Rolling Stone*. "I remember when I was young, this is serious, I read an article by Fats Domino which influenced me. He said, 'You should never sing lyrics out very clearly.'" (In other words, Leonard was not crazy when he shouted, "What the fuck is he saying?") Jagger also said he agreed with the ministers who worried about the nefarious influence of black music—the sound of Chess remade the world. "Music is one of the things that changes society," he explained. "That old thing of not letting white children listen to black music is true, 'cause if you want white children to remain what they are, they mustn't."

Leonard never understood the white bands inspired by the Chess label. When they came to the studio on pilgrimage, he dismissed them as freaks. Here we have Leonard facing the future and what does he do? He turns away, or simply cannot see it. Muddy Waters, Chuck Berry, Howlin' Wolf, this was something he saw and understood when few others did. These men and their music were authentic and so were recognized by Leonard, who himself never wanted to be anything but what he was. But these English bands, with their accents and eyeliner and hair spray, were something he simply could not understand. They were not real. It was a future he would have no part of. The greeting and coddling of these musicians was accordingly turned over to Marshall, who was a product of his time as much as he was a product of Leonard. On Michigan Avenue, when Marshall was

The Mike Douglas Show, *1971: John Lennon jams with Chuck Berry, the inventor of the scene. The mojo crackles between them like the radio between towns.* (© Jeff Albertson/Corbis)

in his convertible with Brian Jones, the Rolling Stones guitarist, Jones's long blond hair tossing in the wind, someone shouted, *Get lost, faggot!*

For Blues musicians, the appearance of hugely popular white bands from Britain was a mixed blessing—these bands brought attention to a music that until then had been ignored. Their popularity would coax many of the legends who had vanished in the first days of Rock & Roll out of retirement. In 1965, when the Stones were asked to appear on *Shindig,* a TV variety show, they said they would appear only if Howlin' Wolf was also asked. He was, and he created one of the great artifacts of Chicago Blues. But the success of the white bands would also suggest to the bluesmen the unfairness of the setup. Someone like Jimmy Rogers, who navigated most of the territory traversed by the Stones, made nothing compared with the money even mediocre bands from Britain made. "Which is why black people resent America," Phil Spector told *Rolling Stone.* "They are the most commercially imitated people, write and sing the most commercial music, yet are the least talked about and the most oppressed."

Muddy had his own regrets, but they tended to be more about legacy—he sensed this great art of his people had been lost. "I think to myself how these white kids was sitting down and playing the blues that my black kids was bypassing," he said. "And it is a hell of thing to think about."

IT IS WRONG to say these bands from Britain were no more than tribute bands or rip-off artists, though many of them started that

way. The first records made by the Rolling Stones are Muddy
Waters reprinted in a loopy, bubblegum font—the band was still
gearing up. It reminds me of Ralph Ellison copying Hemingway
sentences in *Invisible Man,* powering up on the report of the other
man's words: "In the fall the war was always there, but we did not
go to it anymore." The Stones were the best of these bands, but
there were dozens of others who came and went, hit and vanished, back to school, into advertising, production. Asher &
Gordon, The Dave Clark Five, The Turtles, Herman's Hermits—
so many bad songs, so many memories trapped in amber. In the
end, the music created its own imitators and its own followers
and its own reality. If you formed a group in the midsixties, you
were probably imitating the Beatles or the Stones even as those
bands were imitating Muddy Waters and Willie Dixon. This is
what Bruce Springsteen meant when he said the first Chuck Berry
guitar lick he ever heard was in a Keith Richards song. In this
way, the music slipped its antecedents and Chess lost its groove.
In this way, time moved on.

It was a terrible irony—well, maybe that's not the right term.
Maybe it's just the sort of absurdity faced by many people if they
live long enough. Because of the success of his work, Muddy
Waters attracted imitators; because of the success of those imitators, which had everything to do with the power of Muddy's
music, he was, twenty years after he pioneered the electric Blues,
urged to copy the copies made of his music. It was as if Carlo
Gambino had been told to carry himself more like Marlon Brando
in *The Godfather. Carlo, no one thinks you're as believable as
Brando!* Muddy had created a world in which Muddy himself

was a stranger. To stay relevant, or so it was felt, he would have to react to this moment. The classic example of this is *Electric Mud,* an album recorded in 1968 at the insistence of Marshall Chess. It's as if Marshall locked Muddy in a studio with a wah-wah pedal and said, *Don't come out until you've made a record.*

Muddy grumbled but went along, willing to compromise for a shot at the big time. In the short run, the record hit. In the long run, it was a fiasco, the artifact most mentioned to suggest the demise of a great label, a classic example of the artist twisted to the monetary fancy of the businessman. It is considered by purists the worst Blues record ever made—an overstatement, surely, an emotional reaction by fans who could not stand to see Muddy look silly. It was Superman covered in kryptonite, which is just a metaphor for the good man weakened by a world of shit. *Electric Mud* was a response to the psychedelic moment, that embarrass-ing tide that swelled and ebbed, scattering the beach in debris. Muddy retooled some of his hits ("Honest I Do," "Mannish Boy") with the tricks of the day. Most telling is track three: Muddy cov-ering the Stones' "Let's Spend the Night Together," which itself is just a much weaker version of the old Muddy Waters hit, "I Just Wanna Make Love to You." The difference in the lyrics—the Willie Dixon tune is up front and no fucking around, whereas the Stones tune is, you know, *let's spend the night together? OK, let's!*—tells all you need to know about the relationship between the music of Chess and the new music that grew out of it. "That *Electric Mud* record was dogshit," Muddy says in the biography *The Mojo Man.* "But when it came out, it started selling like wild, but then they started sending them back. They said, 'This can't be Muddy Waters with all this shit going on, all this wha-wha and fuzztone.' "

Marshall tried hard in those years to return Muddy to the mainstream. His most interesting effort was *Fathers and Sons,* an album, recorded a year after *Electric Mud,* that featured Blues classics remade by Muddy and pianist Otis Spann playing with two of the white kids they most influenced: Paul Butterfield, who plays harp in the style of Little Walter, and Mike Bloomfield, who plays guitar as Jimmy Rogers turned into Rock & Roll. To me, Bloomfield is of special interest because Bloomfield is where the life of kids like Marshall overlap with the life of men like Muddy—where, in a sense, Marshall becomes Muddy. In another era, Bloomfield would probably have pursued a career in Classical Music or Jazz, or else would have become a record man in the style of Jerry Wexler—but now, mostly because of the success of labels like Chess, he was free to live a Rock & Roll life, which is the Blues life on speed. "I knew Mike Bloomfield since I was a kid," Marshall told me. "We were from the same town and both went to New Trier high school. One day, Bloomfield comes up to me, and this was before anyone around there knew much about the Blues, and says, 'Hey man, I know all about Chess records and Chuck Berry and Muddy Waters.' His family was wealthy, Bloomfield Industries, restaurant supply, saltshakers. He lived in a big house on Sheridan Road. He had a red guitar and was trying to learn Chuck Berry guitar lines. I went to the studio and swiped one of Muddy's slides and gave it to Mike. It was his first bottleneck."

When he was fifteen, Bloomfield, who had a towering Dylanesque head of hair—the term is *Jew-fro*—and deep-set eyes and was handsome in the way of a suburban kid trying to look downtown, began hanging around the South Side clubs. Buddy Guy, who had a contract with Chess, played it cool whenever Bloomfield came around. "You wouldn't see a white face in those clubs unless it was a cop," he explained. By arranging *Father and Sons,* Marshall was doing a bit of social engineering. He was saying to Muddy, even if Muddy did not agree, *these are your sons—this is your legacy.* Unlike the British rockers, with their knighthoods and estates and ponies, Bloomfield, the rich kid from the North Shore, actually lived the Blues life to the end. In 1965, he played guitar on "Like a Rolling Stone" for Bob Dylan, and also on the rest of *Highway 61 Revisited.* He went on to record a dozen albums, with bands and by himself, many of them straight Blues. Then he dropped out of the business. He was, in fact, scoring porno films. In 1977, he came back with the album *If You Love These Blues, Play Them As You Please,* which was nominated for a Grammy Award. In 1978, he died of an overdose. He was thirty-four, about the same age as Robert Johnson at his death, which, of course, means nothing.

All this is the third act of the electric Blues, the moment when the last of the legacy is stripped away, when the old-timers are forced to ask the question, How do you operate in a world that has left your body but taken your soul? To me, the apex of this moment was reached in 1974, when Muddy Waters, the inventor of the sound, was hired as entertainment at Mick Jagger's twenty-ninth birthday party.

6

The Record Man
Pays for Our Sins

By the midsixties, the position of Leonard Chess had become increasingly difficult. With the advance of the civil rights movement, and with its increasing radicalization, and with the appearance of Malcolm X and the Black Panthers and a nation of separatists, outfits like Chess, which recorded black artists and sold mostly to the black community and yet were owned by white businessmen, were coming to be seen as a big part of the problem. For the Chess family, this was the age of visits from operation PUSH, the civil rights organization established, in Chicago, by the young Jesse Jackson. Each week, some agent from the operation showed up with a grievance, soliciting a "contribution." And there were other payments, tens of thousands given to the NAACP and the ACLU and all sorts of organizations, some made because Leonard felt the cause just—he was, in fact, an early and vocal supporter of the movement—some made to stave off the inevitable. At a public event, Leonard handed Martin Luther King a check for two thousand dollars. In June 1967, he told the *Chicago Daily News* he gave to the black cause because "I made my money on the Negro and now I want to spend it on him." It was the last days of the old order. You could feel it like the squeeze Leonard felt years before as the white owner of a nightclub in the ghetto. It wasn't just Chess, of course. It was Jubilee and Atlantic and King, all the independents that, with each turn of the screw, came to be seen as exploiters. "It was getting to the end of that era of whites owning black businesses," said Marshall. "I had so many fucking arguments with Jesse Jackson when he was a young minister. He would try and get us to hire more black executives. And there was major pressure."

Leonard had the ability—maybe it's an especially Jewish ability and maybe it comes from a historical fear—to spot thunderheads from a distance. He knew he would need an escape from race music, a chopper out as the city fell, and began preparing as early as 1959, when, for two hundred and sixty thousand dollars he bought WTAC, a radio station in Flint, Michigan. From there, he continued to build. This was to be his future. Before he died, he would own five radio stations and had just bought his first television station—his first because it seems clear he intended to build a network. In 1963, he bought WVON, a black Chicago radio station that Leonard built into one of the top stations in the city. At first, this station was seen mostly as an auxiliary to the record label. "Leonard told Otis Spann [who worked as a DJ at the station] to play Koko Taylor's new song for three days and so many orders came in he had to press it just like popping your fingers," Willie Dixon wrote in his autobiography.

Leonard Chess in the 1960s. Where others continued to see a market, he saw a mob. It was time to get out. (© Michael Ochs Archives.com)

And yet, radio was more than just a way to sell records—it was a way into a new life and it grew into an obsession. In it, Leonard found an excitement he had not known since his early days in the music business. He was soon spending more time at WVON than at the record label, his Cadillac tacking back and forth across the city. In these years, he helped invent modern black radio, replacing the old canned format with news and live coverage. The station became a Voice in the Movement. Martin Luther King was often on the air; so were Elijah Mohammed and Malcolm X and Thurgood Marshall. The station's call letters stood for "voice of the Negro." At a time when black audiences were spoken to almost exclusively by white broadcasters, all the on-air personnel at WVON were black. The off-air personnel, however, were white, a fact not unnoticed by the reverends. While Leonard said to himself, *Look at all the good I'm doing for the black community,* the leaders of that community said, *Why is the biggest Negro station in the city owned by a Polish Jew?*

In a sense, the black artists and the white record men had been joined in a marriage, a wedding of outsiders. And though their needs overlapped, they were not in the end the same needs. This became clear in the sixties. "These performers were increasingly used as spearheads and symbols in the black movement," Bob Krasnow told me. "They were supposed to show the world they would no longer be manipulated by whites." All of a sudden, you were no longer dealing person to person. You were dealing symbol to symbol. Group to group. In even the smallest exchange, it was every white man talking to every black man. "And it all came down to this," said Krasnow: "Who is fucking who? And what is Atlantic paying in royalties? And what about Roulette? And what about Chess?" In most cases, the anger of the artists—and it was a very angry time—was met with incomprehension. *We're selling records, ain't we? You got a new car, don't you?* To Leonard it was clear the rupture would come, and it did come, on April 4, 1968, when Martin Luther King was killed in Memphis. In Chicago, five days of rioting ensued. Nine people died. Mayor Daley asked Leonard to use his radio station to calm the black community. For record men, this was the big moment, the grand bow out, the serving of papers, the filing for divorce.

Bob Krasnow was in Los Angeles with James Brown when the ghetto started to burn. "We had gone to do this TV show. We were staying at the Continental Hyatt House or the Riot House as we called it. We turn on our television and L.A. is on fire. People are walking through busted windows with TVs. So the next day James says, 'I can't have any white people around me anymore.' Are you fucking kidding me? 'No, man, you're fired, gone.' And I'm saying, 'Come on, James, did I kill Martin Luther King? I mean, can't we just be two people? Can't we just be me and you?' He says, 'No, motherfucker. Can't do it anymore.' This was the seminal moment for the business—the white guys and the black guys, it ended that night, it was all over, man."

The age of payback, as rife with colorful episodes as a book on pirates. For many record men, it was the last year on the old block. The neighborhood, as they say in Bensonhurst, had gone punk. "There was something sick in the air," Jerry Wexler writes in *Rhythm & the Blues: A Life in American Music*. "An anger, a frustration, a tension that had already reached the boiling points in the inner cities of Newark and Detroit." For the old machers, it was a moment of terrible realization. As Jews, they felt, even as they were ripping off artists, they had a special relationship with the black community. They were, as Jews, on the right side of the big issues by birth. Even when men like Leonard Chess and Jerry Wexler were called names, they stubbornly considered themselves great progressives: in business in the ghetto, employers and partners of blacks, cherishing a music that was beneath the boots of the rest of the country. "I understood prejudice, had seen it my whole life, and always thought I was on the right side," Wexler writes. "As a Jew, I didn't think I identified with the underclass. I *was* the underclass." "In a probably stupid way, we all thought of ourselves as pioneers for black people," Ahmet Ertegun said in *Rhythm & the Blues*. "We were the ones who made the original black records that were covered by white artists—and we were the ones who fought to get the black artists on the air." And now these same men were being told they were, if anything, merely a swarthier take on white, built in the same lab as the rest of the devils.

It was a moment that reached its apogee—if we stick with the divorce metaphor, it was the big fight in front of the kids after which nothing is the same, after which there are only lawyers and alimony and restraining orders—in 1968, four months after Martin Luther King was killed. For the music business, it was the big Tolstoy scene, the players gathered in grand tableau beneath the liquid skies of Miami Beach. The convention of the National Association of Television and Radio Announcers. The Sheraton Four Ambassadors Hotel. The lobby was an aquarium of the counterculture, bell-bottoms, madras shirts, mood rings, sandals, little men in tall shoes, tall men with little spoons around their necks. The leaders of the civil rights movement were there: Jesse Jackson and Coretta Scott King. But the scene was quickly taken over by a gang of heavies—they blew through the ballrooms like a sirocco, punishing businessmen and label heads, shouting and cursing, collecting in the name of the oppressed.

This group called itself the Fairplay Committee. Made up of street toughs from New York, it was led by a man who dressed like a sharpie from the Harlem Renaissance, someone in a painting or a poem, candy-colored suits and shiny leather shoes. His fingers were compared in size and texture to sausages. His name was Dino Woodart, but everyone called him Boom Boom—because he could not get through a sentence without saying the word *boom*. He had been a boxer and had sparred with Sugar Ray Robinson, and his years in the ring had left him punchy; *boom* was the only word that never let him down. It meant everything. It meant yeah, and nah, and watch out, and don't fuck with the black man. *Boom, you take millions from the black man. Boom! Now you gotta pay. Boom! You don't pay. Boom! Boom!* The committee vowed to avenge black musicians by threatening white record men and collecting payoffs, which went mostly to benefit the members of the Fairplay Committee. "Like if people had a problem," Woodart is quoted as saying in *Music Man: Ahmet Ertegun, Atlantic Records and the Triumph of Rock & Roll,* by Dorothy Wade and Justine Picarole. "We would stand up for them."

"It was just old-fashioned take what you can get blackmail," wrote Wexler. "Suspicious characters hitting on label and station owners under the guise of concerned citizens. Hoodlums camouflaging extortion with the rhetoric of the Movement."

The *New York Times* called the convention "Mayhem in Miami." A record man said, "There was blood on the floors." It replicated, in miniature, the fear that was spreading through the music business, that would, in the end, drive most of the independent record men into the arms of the corporations—big companies that would then quickly brush off small-time operators like Boom Boom, a lesson for the heavies. (Woodart wound up back in New York, where he is a reverend at the Abyssinian Baptist Church in Harlem.) On the first night of the convention, the great saxophone player King Curtis grabbed Wexler by the arm and said, "We're getting the fuck out of here."

"Why?"

"Someone is after you with a gun. You're marked."

In his book, Wexler, who, even in the teeth of the action, cannot help but appreciate a good lyric, writes, "Another brother materialized—blues singer Titus Turner (who wrote the ingenious 'Around the World,' for Little Willie John, with the classic line 'If I don't love you baby, grits ain't groceries, eggs ain't poultry'). With Titus showing his piece, they whisked me out of the auditorium in nothing flat."

Later that night, Jerry Wexler was hung in effigy.

Worse still was the fate of Marshall Sehorn, who worked at Fury Records in New Orleans and who is credited, rather suspiciously, with writing some of the trademark songs of Elmore James. Sehorn carried a gun, which, one evening, as he showered in his hotel suite, he slung across a chair. When he looked up, it was gone. He put on a towel and got out of the shower. Four men crowded into the bathroom. One of them had Sehorn's gun, and was waving it around. Another said, "We don't want anymore white niggers"—a symbolic bit of dialogue that indicts Sehorn, but also Wexler and Ertegun and Chess and a whole generation of record men. A thug reached under Sehorn's towel and crunched his nuts—how else to describe it? He said, "This is for all the black girls you screwed." And the gun came around and *boom, boom, out go the lights.* "These guys were taking everything out on whites like Marshall Sehorn, who had always been a champion of black artists and black music," Ahmet Ertegun said in *Music Man.* "To pick on a little guy like that, who never made any money and fought for the music all his life, is unfair. When things like that happen, you lose your appetite for continuing in this thing—when the people you think are your allies . . ."

Leonard knew it was time to get out—it's what made him a great businessman. He had seen a market where others had seen only a horde, and now he could see a mob where others continued to see a market. From that moment, he had his ears open and his feelers out—he was convinced it was *get out now with something or be forced out later with nothing.* Why did he reach such a conclusion? At this point, it is appropriate to do a quick fade to four years earlier, 1964, an episode that must have convinced Leonard that the stream of commerce he was riding was in fact carrying him toward a Niagara.

Leonard was home in Glencoe when the phone rang: *There's been a break-in at the studio. You need to get down here.* Leonard roared through the canopy of trees—in the fall, everything on the North Shore is golden—and emerged on the South Side, endless blocks of the slum, streets running on toward the prairie. 2120 looked okay. He parked and walked to the door. Four men came out of the alley. *Good, maybe they know what's going on.* Before he can ask, they are on him, punching, kicking, rifling his pockets—maybe even then, he realizes the whole thing is a setup, an ambush. He has been lured from his house to be beaten and robbed in front of his office, on the street where he made his name, not for any political reason but simply because here is a white man in the ghetto and as such is sure to be loaded with cash. Leonard saw himself as a member of the community, but these men saw him as an outsider, a dollar sign, a Jew. It was a symbolic beating. It was, in the Krasnow sense, every black man raining blows on every white man in the record business. It was the kind of ugly beating that can never be captured on film— and no one ever tries. The sound of such a beating, the grunts and moans and shouts, would turn an onlooker into an accomplice and convince a viewer that these people, perpetrators and victim, represent the true nature of life—vicious and fallen, and civilization is a lie. How could you survive such a beating without losing your faith in the world?

LEONARD CHESS SOLD his label in 1968. He had owned the company for twenty years. In that time, he had made millions, assembled the greatest catalogue in the history of the Blues, reinvented popular music twice, first by ushering in the electric Blues, then by ushering in Rock & Roll, and had helped create the style and mystique and legend of the modern record man. And now it was over. The majors had moved in and driven up the costs of recording sessions and contracts. What the majors did not poach would be stripped away by the Fairplay Committees of the world. As far as Leonard was concerned, he was exiting at the top of the Ferris wheel. He made his deal quickly, quietly. Marshall did not find out until it was done. One afternoon, the old man just calls from his car phone—who even knew they had car phones back then?—and says, "Phil and I talked. We decided to sell the company to GRT." To Marshall, Leonard might as well have said: *Phil and I talked. We decided to give away your birthright.*

"It's a good deal," said Leonard. "And it's the right time."

"What am I supposed to do?" asked Marshall. "I was raised to be a record man."

"Hey, Marshall, you're gonna get a million bucks. Start your own label."

In the reassuring voice of a strong father, which almost always turns out to be wrong, Leonard then said, "Don't worry, Marshall. You're going to be okay."

Leonard's attorney had connected him with GRT: General Recording Tape. Probably few have heard of it today, but in the 1960s it was a company on the make, a founder of Silicon Valley, at the forefront of the new technology—one of those now defunct concerns that, for a brief moment, seemed set to take over the world. Its owners pioneered, along with the Ampex Corporation, the cassette and eight-track tape, which, in the music business, were the first important hardware innovations since the invention of the long-playing record. GRT controlled the patent on this technology and so grew by great bounds, signing deals with major labels, converting thousands of recordings into tape. Yet you cannot hold a long-term patent on a container—you can own the rights to the cola, but not the can—and so the company had only short-term contracts that would soon expire. Most of the record labels, it was assumed, would then build their own plants.

GRT was therefore scrambling for product, content, something to put on tape. Hence the deal with Chess. In one move, GRT would acquire both new releases and a tremendous backlist.

The heads of GRT did not much care what kind of record company they were buying—what kind of cola, Pepsi or Jolt—as long as they had something to put in the cans. Negotiations dragged on. GRT complained about Chess's "Jewish greed." Leonard complained about GRT's "Gentile mentality." The GRT executives were in fact nerds, chip freaks and computer geeks, a premonition of the next fifty years. Marshall called them "Stanford men . . . the West Coast version of Harvard assholes." Leonard should have known such men would never understand the mercurial nature of the record business. It was a collision of cultures, uncool finding itself in sudden control of the coolest thing on earth. The artists at Chess were "particularly concerned when GRT sent some accountants over," Dick LaPalm, a producer at the label, said in *I Am the Blues*. "I thought the Chess guys were going to kill this one accountant."

Leonard Chess considered his deal a classic outsmarting of Gentile mentality, but he was wrong. Leonard and Phil were to be paid 6.5 million dollars plus twenty thousand shares of GRT stock. But GRT only had to come up with 4.7 million in cash. The rest was to be owed with interest. It was not a good price even for the time. A few years later, Ahmet Ertegun and Jerry Wexler sold Atlantic Records to Warner Brothers for twenty million dollars—and even that came to seem like a trip to the cleaners. Jerry Wexler later said it was the greatest mistake of his career. In the mid-1990s, Jimmy Iovine, who founded Interscope

Records, a hip-hop label not even in the same league as Chess, sold out to a major label for over two hundred million dollars. In other words, Leonard—maybe because he had built his label from scratch, maybe because there were no points of reference, maybe because he was overanxious to sell—did not stop to consider just what he had. There was the tremendous backlist, probably the best in the history of the Blues and early Rock & Roll: the top-flight roster of current stars; the mechanism of distribution and advertising; and also the name, which was invaluable—the trademark and social power of Chess. Sharp as he was, Leonard misjudged the situation. He misjudged GRT. Atlantic at least sold to a company involved in the arts, and so that label continues to this day—Ertegun still has an office. But GRT was in trouble from the moment the documents were signed. The brothers would never receive the money they were owed, and the stock was restricted—it could not be sold for several years. "When the deal was made, the stock was trading at seventeen dollars," Marshall told me. "By the time I was able to sell, I got $1.78. My mother got zero. She waited too long."

For Leonard, this deal should have been the big payout, but it was a disaster. Within five years, the market had stripped away what it took a lifetime to accumulate. *Oh, Leonard, you were a sharpie all your life, moving score to score, outfoxing your artists and producers, never missing a trick, never missing a beat, preying on record men and distributors, strong-arming DJs, fighting over the price of a bus ticket or a bottle of whiskey, but when you finally got to the table with the corporate boys you never stood a chance. You were winning all night, but you lost on the very last hand.*

The executives at GRT said they wanted Chess Records to continue as before, with Leonard at the helm, calling the shots, churning out the hits, but of course things started to change right away. In the corporate world, the only thing as important as money is control: which meant no dope smoking in the back rooms, no black guys hanging out for no reason, no shouting in the halls, no *Get that fucking cocksucker on the fucking phone,* no *Hey, Marshall, run out and get Wolf a bottle of applejack.* Within a few months of the sale, 2120 South Michigan had been overrun by auditors, managers, accountants, suit-wearing Nancy boys, number crunchers, scolders and shushers, *actual library-style shushers,* who wanted to go over those numbers again, keep it quiet in the lobby, contain and control all that noise and action that might seem like chaos but was in fact the rhythm section of the label. Without it, the song had no drive. It was like trying to run a crime family without all those aimless espresso drinking hours at the social club. Leonard responded by staying away, coming in late, leaving early, spending more and more time at WVON. He was concerned only with securing a place for Marshall, protecting him from the corporation. "It was like cancer from the moment GRT arrived," Marshall told me. "They were sending me to budget meetings. Chess was never run that way, we never had budget meetings, never thought about how many hits are we *going* to have. We just hoped and kept trying. Now it was a public corporation, and we had to submit shit to the shareholders."

The artists responded by steering clear, staying away, meeting somewhere else, and the mood sagged and the label died. Those who built Chess speak of this moment in that tone you reserve for the worst facts of growing old—the way everything you once loved changes, or fades away.

"The recording sessions became foreign, full of red tape," Chuck Berry said later, "permission from other departments, as opposed to the family-type small-business style of the earlier sessions."

The majors, the big corporations, had at last gotten the word, *There's gold in them there hills,* and so rolled in with their big money and big contracts and armies of accountants and marketers. Yet by their very presence, these companies killed what they came to capture, the creativity and freedom and energy of the small labels. They were like that clumsy idiot in the Steinbeck book who crushes the puppy he tries to love. At best, something of these labels might be preserved with a kind of taxidermy, a few machers at the long table in the board meeting, a classic name preserved as a stylish meaningless imprint, like an antelope head on the wall of the New York Athletic Club. Over time, men like Hy Weiss and Jerry Wexler were driven out or changed into office creatures, into boardroom brinksmen, hustlers removed from the music and the street. The majors, not able to compete, had simply bought out or co-opted the independents. The business was soon as stolid and boring as it had been before Chess and Atlantic and Roulette, before the war, before the explosion of new music. To the bands who couldn't get a hearing, it was corporate rock, major labels too timid and slow to reckon with the next break of the wave. Whenever a new music does emerge (grunge, hip-hop), a group of independents appears to record it, and then quickly vanishes, bought out, chased away. It's the story of America: the creep of the corporation, the death of the cow-boy, the controlled explosions that brought down the old gang-ster hotels in Vegas. And Meyer Lansky is looking for asylum in the Jewish Homeland, and Vito Genovese is living in Naples, and the last of the old shore places have closed down.

As Hy Weiss told me, "Whatever brings the money into the bank. Nothing is disreputable if you are cashing the check."

By 1969, Leonard was out of the company. There had been a struggle for control. According to Nadine Cohodas, Alan Bailey, the president of GRT, said, "I did not look on Marshall as being equipped to replace Leonard. In fact, I felt he never would have that capability." Marshall said to the corporate bosses in essence, *I run the company, or I walk.* The bosses made the smart play: they elevated Marshall, which would prevent a mass exodus, placate artists and producers, give a false sense of continuity. It had been a dream for Marshall, but now it was hollow, another label dying in the sticks—steering wheel not even connected to the axle. The corporate board sent him to the American Management Association to learn to be an executive: the handshake, the walk. Phil Chess was given a ceremonial role. He would soon retire. He later sold WVON for nine million dollars and a smaller station, which became WLUP, for 5.25 million. Marshall headed Chess for less than a year. He was a front, waving in the window as GRT moved the furniture out the back. He quit in 1970 and went trav-eling, sleeping on the couches of friends, including Jann Wenner, the founder of *Rolling Stone* magazine. He wanted to start a new label. "I had Boz Skaggs," he told me. "He helped change my head, because he was one of the first psychedelic trippers, and he told me about the books by Carlos Castenada, which blew my mind."

Marshall's plans soon came apart. He fell into a funk. "It was like I'd been training for an athletic event all my life and they canceled it a month before the Olympics," he said. He took a job with the Rolling Stones—probably the band was less interested in Marshall than in his name, draping themselves in the glory that had been Chess. He was soon back on his own, bouncing scene to scene, years rushing past. When I interviewed Marshall in New York—he is a lean, handsome man with warm eyes—he seemed a figure of regret. *Don't worry, Marshall, everything will be okay.* For a time, he was back in the studio, having finally started his own label. He called it CZYZ, the pre-American spelling of the family name, a choice that suggests the great difference between Marshall, the kid from the suburbs, and his father, who was forever fleeing the old country.

For GRT, Chess was ultimately more trouble than it was worth. And so the terrible calculation was made: the parts, which could be sold, were worth more than the whole. (GRT was having its own trouble—the market was moving away from it.) In 1970, Chess Records, which had become little more than a name, was moved from Chicago to New York. Within a year, it was bankrupt. Contracts canceled, employees let go, artists released. The catalogue was sold. In 1986, after many of the records had gone out of print, it was bought by MCA. Classics were re-released and royalties paid, but the company itself had become a memory. 2120 South Michigan had been condemned. When workmen came through, they found hundreds of records—scratched up LPs by Koko Taylor and Jimmy Rogers and Little Walter and John Lee Hooker and Howlin' Wolf and Chuck Berry and Bo

Diddley and Robert Nighthawk and Little Milton—left like garbage at a picnic site. Some were carried off by the workers, most were destroyed.

Chess Records pressed more than music—it pressed the mystique and style of Rock & Roll. Artists like Muddy Waters and Bo Diddley invented the sound, the swagger: Diddley sings, "I walked forty-seven miles of barbed wire, I wear a cobra snake for a necktie." Leonard invented the image and style of the record executive, the cigar-smoking presence behind the music. It was an accidental invention, Leonard being Leonard, but there is no way to look at postwar social history without looking at Chess. He created an image as archetypal and American as the woodsman or logger or city desk editor. The record man—rough and vulgar and comical and irritating and cheap and rude, but when you shook his hand, you knew you had really met someone.

LEONARD WAS SUPERSTITIOUS and was afraid if he signed a will he would die, so he didn't sign a will, and he died anyway. As he was leaving the Chess office in the fall of 1968, an accountant told him there was trouble with unpaid bills. GRT was pulling cash from the label to cover debts elsewhere—eating the cake from the middle. Leonard went as crazy as Leonard could go, up into the red, face flashing like a traffic light. His chest rose, his arms tightened. He stormed into the office of the corporate manager. He shouted, *What the fuck is this about, we don't pay our fucking bills? Look, you fuck. It's still my name on the door and I pay my fucking bills.* He stormed into the street. He had not been this angry in years—you never feel as alive as when you are in a fury. Time slows, objects etch themselves in your memory. His secretary chased him, sat next to him as he got into his Cadillac. He roared off. The brick buildings, the bleached avenues, all that clean light reflecting off storefronts and bumpers, the great midwestern city, middle of the continent, so far from Poland, from the past, from history. Leonard looked out at it and started to say something but then grabbed his chest and fell across the wheel. He had suffered a massive coronary. He was fifty-two. His secretary dug frantically through his bag for his pills. It was too late. He was already dead. He crossed two lanes of traffic and hit a parked car.

Sources

This book is a version of a story I've been telling since tenth grade, usually in my room, which, thanks to my brother flying off to college, was, Greg Brady style, in the attic, where I sat cross-legged in front of the stereo, books and records scattered before me, reading passages, quoting lyrics, using whatever was at hand to make the case: not only does this song rock, it also has something big to tell us. I've here employed an adult version of this same method, drawing on CDs, books, and interviews.

First, those books which I owe special acknowledgment, which I learned from, relied on, referred to:

Spinning Blues into Gold, the excellent book by Nadine Cohodas, which offers the only full-scale treatment of the Chess brothers
Deep Blues, the legendary riff by Robert Palmer
The Land Where Blues Began, by Alan Lomax
Stomping the Blues, by Albert Murray

The Voice of the Blues: Classic Interviews from Living Blues Magazine, edited by Jim O'Neil and Amy Van Singel

Chuck Berry: The Biography, by John Collis

Chess Records, by John Collis

The Country Blues, by Samuel B. Charters

Chicago Blues, by Mike Rowe

Muddy Waters: The Mojo Man, by Sandra B. Tooze

Rhythm & the Blues: A Life in American Music, by Jerry Wexler and David Ritz

Rage to Survive: The Etta James Story, by Etta James and David Ritz

The Rolling Stone Book of Interviews

I Am the Blues: The Willie Dixon Story, by Willie Dixon with Don Snowden

Big Beat Heat: Alan Freed and the Early Years of Rock & Roll, by John Jackson

Music Man: Ahmet Ertegun, Atlantic Records and the Triumph of Rock & Roll, by Dorothy Wade and Justine Picardie

Crosstown Traffic: Jimi Hendrix & Post-War Pop, by Charles Shaar Murray

Blues People, by Leroi Jones (Amiri Baraka)

Music & Technology in the Twentieth Century, edited by Hans-Joachim Braun

Rough Mix, by Jimmy Bowen and Jim Jerome

Gem of the Prairie: An Informal History of the Chicago Underworld, by Herbert Asbury

Searching for Robert Johnson, a mysterious sliver of a book by Peter Guralnick

The voice of this book comes from the record men themselves, from dozens of people I spoke to for this story, and also in the course of ten or so years of journalistic adventures in the music business, as a contributing editor at *Rolling Stone* magazine and as a screenwriter, researching a script about the industry which I co-wrote with Martin Scorsese and Mick Jagger. Interviews with, among others: Marshall Chess, Ahmet Ertegun, David Geffen, Bob Krasnow, Joe Smith, Lou Adler, Bob Gibson, Jerry Moss, Marty Asher, Irving Azoff, Val Azzoil, Jeff Ayeroff, Jimmy Bowen, Doug Morris, Lyor Cohen, Russell Simmons, Danny Goldberg, Julie Rifkin, Artie Mogull, Susan Blond, Greg Geller, Hy Weiss, Seymour Stein, Gary Gersh, Bruce Flohr, Jimmy Iovine, Phil Walden, Richard Perry, Eddie Rosenblatt, Al Teller, Sylvia Rhone, Bob Merlis, Mario Medius, Tommy Lipuma, John Kalodner, Mel Lewinter, Steve Baker, Dick Asher, Mick Jagger, Keith Richards, Charlie Watts, Ron Wood, Darryl Jones, Chuck Lavelle, and Roger McGuinn.

But for me, the greatest moment was when I went back to Glencoe, Illinois—where Leonard raised his family and where I grew up about two generations later—address in hand, searching the streets for the Chess house, which, in the end, I found just a few doors away from the red-brick Tudor where I was raised. In other words, while I had been holding my tenth-grade attic symposiums on the torturous course of the Blues and early Rock & Roll, I had (unknowingly) been no more than three hundred yards from one of the great landmarks of the story. But that, of course, is the essence of all this American music: familiar yet strange, just down the street and a world away.

Suggested Listening

I recently spent a morning with Marshall Chess, talking about music and what he was up to now. A wall in his office—he runs Arc Music, the publishing company attatched to Chess, in Manhattan—is lined with pictures from the old days, one showing the preteen Marshall on the beach in a sailor's hat with Leonard holding his hand, a side trip in the course of one of the record man's swings through the South. Marshall spoke about his Uncle Phil, who, in his mid-eighties, lives in Arizona, where he has become deeply involved with horses. A few years ago, Phil owned a horse that ran in the Kentucky Derby. Marshall told me it was important that people realize how crucial Phil was to the success of the label. Phil was a great businessman but also a great record man, responsible for some of the most powerful recording work done in the modern era. Leonard stood out front, Marshall told me, "but none of it would have been possible without Phil."

At one point, Marshall turned on his computer and opened his iTunes, his library of MP3s, and I thought, wow, there is an interesting artifact—the music collection of Marshall Chess, the son of the great record man. In recent years, Marshall has been working with his own son, Jemar, teaching him the business, the two of them, father and son, or, depending on your point of view, son and grandson, traveling, not through the American South but through Italy, in search of Italian hip-hop artists. They run sessions in a recording studio in Florence.

I asked Marshall to name some of his favorite records from Chess, which readers of this book might want to listen to. He said it would be tough to narrow all that work down to a few sides, but, the next morning, he sent along this list.

Chuck Berry: *The Great 28* (great current compilation)
Howlin' Wolf: *Moanin in the Moonlight*
Bo Diddly: *Bo Diddly* (first LP)
Sonny Boy Williamson: *Down and Out Blues*
Muddy Waters: *Folk Singer*; *Fathers and Sons*; *Electric Mud*;
    and all best-of CDs and box sets
Etta James: *At Last*
Rotary Connection: *Rotary Connection*
In addition, all the CDs released by MCA to mark the label's fiftieth anniversary.

To that, I would add some of my own favorites, Chess and otherwise.

Charley Patton: *The Best of Charley Patton*

Robert Johnson: *The Complete Recordings*

Little Walter: *The Chess 50th Anniversary Collection*

Koko Taylor: *The Chess 50th Anniversary Collection*

Jimmy Rogers: *The Chess 50th Anniversary Collection*

Elvis Presley: *The Sun Sessions*

The Ventures: *Live in Japan*

The Rolling Stones: *Exile on Main Street*; *Sticky Fingers*;
   Beggars Banquet

Bob Dylan: *Highway 61 Revisited*; *Love & Theft*

The White Stripes: *Elephant*

But really, when it comes to a lot of the old Chess records, you can't go wrong, because they all grow out of the same tradition, and so are like ramps on to a common highway, where every road leads to every other road, and every other road takes you pretty much wherever you want to go.

Acknowledgments

Acknowledgment is gratefully made to the following sources:

"Boom, Boom, Out Go the Lights." Words and Music by Stan Lewis. Copyright © 1957 (renewed) Arc Music Corporation (BMI). All rights reserved. International copyright secured. Used by permission.

"Bring It On Home" by Willie Dixon. Copyright © 1964, 1965 (renewed) Hoochie Coochie Music (BMI)/Administered by BUG. All rights reserved. Used by permission.

"Cross Road Blues" (a/k/a "Crossroads") by Robert Johnson. Written by Robert Johnson. Copyright © 1990 Lehsem II, LLC/Claud L. Johnson.

"Downbound Train" by Chuck Berry. Copyright © Isalee Music Publishing Company. All rights reserved. Used by permission.

"Here Comes Your Man" by the Pixies. Written by Black

Index

Page numbers in *italics* refer to illustrations.